THE ALLURE OF CHANEL

PAUL MORAND

THE ALLURE OF CHANEL

Translated from the French by
Euan Cameron

PUSHKIN PRESS
LONDON

English translation © Euan Cameron 2008
Afterword © Euan Cameron 2008

First published in French as
L'Allure de Chanel © Hermann 1976

First published in 2008 by
Pushkin Press
12 Chester Terrace
London N1 4ND

This special illustrated edition first published in 2009

British Library Cataloguing in Publication Data:
A catalogue record for this book is available
from the British Library

ISBN 978 1 906548 10 0

Cover Illustration: Portrait of Gabrielle Chanel Man Ray 1935
© Man Ray Trust ADAGP Paris 2009

Frontispiece: Portrait of Paul Morand 1935
© Rex Features Roger-Viollet

All illustrations are printed with the permission of the copyright holders
Art Direction by Christopher Scott Vann

Set in 13 on 16 Monotype Baskerville
and printed in Great Britain by
TJ International Padstow Cornwall

conqueror.

Cover printed on Conqueror Texture Laid Diamond White 300g
Text pages printed on Conqueror Texture Laid Diamond White 120g

www.pushkinpress.com

THE ALLURE OF
CHANEL

PREFACE

I arrived at rue Cambon for the first time. A New Year's Eve party in 1921, I believe. "You're all invited to Coco's," Misia had said to us; all, that is to say les Six, *our group from Le Boeuf sur le Toit, the young people from Madame Alphonse Daudet's salon, the regulars from the Jean Hugos' studio at the Palais Royal, and those who attended our Saturday evening dinner parties at Darius Milhaud's home. Chanel had not yet conquered Paris; the buffet had been laid out in the fitting rooms which had remained as they were in 1914, rather like a private clinic, in which Mme Langweil's coromandel screens had not yet unfurled their autumn leaves. Apart from her Deauville clients, or some polo players, friends of the Capel whom she had just lost, Chanel was very lonely, very shy, very closely watched; that evening Misia brought along people who would be Chanel's life-long companions, the Philippe Berthelots, Satie, Lifar, Auric, Segonzac, Lipschitz, Braque, Luc-Albert Moreau, Radiguet, Sert, Elise Jouhandeau, Picasso, Cocteau, Cendrars (not Reverdy yet). Their presence alone marked the break with 1914, a past now dismissed, and a path that opened to the future, a future in which bankers would no longer be called Salomon, but Boy, or Lewis, where Satie would not write* Espana, *but* Espagna, *where perfumes would no longer be called* Trèfle incarnate *and* Rêve d'automne, *but would bear a reference number, as convicts do.*

THE ALLURE OF CHANEL

You wouldn't have recognised Chanel's genius; there was nothing yet to suggest her authority, her violent rages, her belligerence, nothing that revealed that character destined for greatness. Only Misia, with her commercial flair, had sensed that Chanel would rise to the top, had detected her serious side behind the frivolity, the precision of her mind and her talent, her uncompromising character. Behind an anxiety enlivened by so many guests, charming in her reticence, and of a shyness that was touching without one quite knowing why—perhaps because of her recent bereavement—Chanel appeared unsure of herself and as if she were questioning her life, no longer believing in happiness: we were bowled over. Did anyone suspect that we were dining, that evening, at the home of the exterminating angel of nineteenth-century style?

"Do you know what 'faner' means?" wrote Mme de Sévigné; 'faner' is to make hay; but it also means to make things wither or lose their freshness; merely by making an appearance, Chanel made the pre-war years wither, she caused Worth or Paquin to wilt. Chanel was a shepherdess; the training track, haymaking, manure, boot leather, saddle soap and the undergrowth smelt good to her. "Our century will have witnessed the revenge of the shepherdesses," says Le Paysan parvenu. *In Chanel's case, it's this ratio of "girls in petticoats and flat shoes" that Marivaux talks about, who are off to brave "the dangers of the city", and prevail over them, with this sturdy appetite for vengeance that unleashes revolutions; Joan of Arc, too, was the revolt of the shepherdess; to quote Marivaux again: "Our century is ushering in the revenge of the shepherds; the peasant is dangerous, I warn you." Chanel is of that breed. She said: "I have given women's bodies back their freedom; that body perspired in formal clothing, beneath the lacework, the corsets, the underwear, the padding"; with Chanel the green countryside regained the upper hand, just as in literature, twenty years earlier, with Colette arriving*

in Paris in the same 'schoolgirl' smock, wearing the same large-bowed neck-tie, the same orphanage slippers. This spirit of revenge would never desert Chanel; it made her cut her beautiful, long hair that got caught in the laces of her corset; it wiped out an entire dream of a lost paradise, which was imaginary in any case, since she had initially loathed and fled from the fabulous childhood that so marked her.

The mystery of complexities! That's where the dark side of Chanel lies, her suffering, her taste for causing harm, her need to castigate, her pride, her strict exactitude, her sarcasm, her destructive anger, the rigidity of a character that blows hot and cold, her abusive, destructive spirit; this belle dame sans merci *would devise poverty for billionaires (all the while dining off gold plates), extravagantly expensive simplicity, seeking out what did not attract attention: the brass on yachts, naval blue and white, the waxed cloth from the hats of Nelson's sailors, the black and white timber frames of the houses in Chester, the slate-grey shade of her lavender fields at Roquebrune, the picnics on the Brenta, those supper parties at La Pausa, without servants, at which one served oneself from plate warmers lined up on the game table. Never was snobbery better directed against oneself.*

The brusqueness of Chanel's character, the precision of her gestures or her phrases, the succinctness of her aphorisms dropped from a heart of flint and delivered in a torrent from the mouth of one of the Eumenides, her way of giving and taking back, of making gifts as if they were insults ("I am sending you these six statues of Venetian Negros," she would ring up and say, "I can't bear them any longer"), everything about her could be traced back to the depths of her frustrated childhood "among peasants who wanted their children to be taller than they themselves" (Bernard Palissy).

In 1900 one did not receive one's 'suppliers', be they Monsieur Doucet or Madame Lanvin; from 1925 onwards, Chanel was not only received, but she made her hosts feel humble, she paid the hotel bills of grand-dukes, and she transformed their Highnesses into chambermaids; this vengeance extended to objects too, as she poured scorn on the sable concealed in a waterproof lining, cropped hairstyles ruthlessly, supplanted silks with the neutrality of jerseys, and replaced bright colours with faded parachutists' uniforms. Might her refusal to marry the Duke of Westminster have been an unexpected way of blotting out Trafalgar and Waterloo? Her hot-tempered pauperism even took pleasure in cheapening precious gems, turning them into common stones; it allowed her to lend her sapphire necklaces to poor girls for a ball (whom she later accused of having stolen them).

Occasionally her nostrils, which were enlarged by a permanent anger, stopped quivering, and it was then that she revealed a certain weariness, and her heart unburdened the secret of a taciturn disposition; but that lasted only a moment, she could not cope without you; the following day, she couldn't stand you any longer. Chanel was Nemesis.

That voice that gushed forth from her mouth like lava, those words that crackled like dried vines, her rejoinders, simultaneously crisp and snappy, a tone that grew more and more peremptory as age took its toll, a tone that was increasingly dismissive, increasingly contradictory, laying irrevocable blame, I heard them all, over entire evenings, in the hotel in St Moritz where I met her in the winter of 1946, unemployed and with nothing to do for the first time in her life, and champing at the bit. She had gone into voluntary exile in the Engadine, unsure whether to return to rue Cambon, and waiting to become wealthy again. She felt both trapped by the past and gripped by time regained, a Guermantes of couture, a Verdurin of an age that was suddenly foreign to her, the De Gaulle years, and black bile flowed from eyes that still sparkled, beneath arched eyebrows increasingly accentuated by eyeliner, like sculpted basalt; Chanel, the volcano from the Auvergne which Paris was mistaken in believing was extinct.

On returning to my bedroom, I scribbled down a few notes from these St Moritz conversations and then thought no more about them; apart from the unforgettable picture of Misia, they were lost to my memory. Moving house in Switzerland last August, I chanced to come across these yellowing pages of thirty years ago. In the meantime, following her death, some very comprehensive books about Chanel had been published, a brilliant novel, as well as the sensitive memoir of a late friendship.

I enjoyed rereading my volatile pages, written on headed notepaper from the Badrutt's Palace, then I felt like sharing my nostalgia with Pierre Berès; he pleaded with me to have them typed out; a slippery slope ... Nothing was written by me; it was all by a ghost, but a ghost who, from beyond the grave, kept up a frantic gallop, her normal pace. Allure, in every sense of the word[1]—the physical and mental rhythms, like the three speeds of a horse that riders refer to; and also, as in hunting, the pace of a stag, to indicate its trail, its course among the leafy boughs and the broken branches; Chanel passed this way, Chanel was there; thirty years is a great forest.

PM [1976]

---

1   In French the word 'allure', as well as having the sense that it has in English of attraction, charm and enticement, also denotes pace and speed of movement. [Tr]

coco orphelie

ALONE

IT IS NOT WITHIN VIEW of my native Puy-de-Dôme that I am speaking to you, this evening, it's in St Moritz, overlooking the Bernina Pass; it's not in our gloomy house where, one day, a proud and inscrutable little girl was taken in, without affection or warmth, that I begin telling you the story of my past life; it's in a brightly lit hotel, where the rich take their pleasure and their laborious rest. But for me, in the Switzerland of today just as in the Auvergne of yesteryear, I have only ever found loneliness.

At the age of six, I am already alone. My mother has just died. My father deposits me, like a millstone, at the house of my aunts, and leaves immediately for an America from which he will never return. An orphan … ever since then, this word has always paralysed me with fear; even now I cannot go past a girls' boarding school and hear people saying "they are orphans", without tears coming to my eyes. Half-a-century has passed, but in the midst of the luxury and happiness enjoyed by the last happy people in a miserable world, I am alone, still alone.

More alone than ever.

These initial remarks are preceded by the word "Alone"; I would not write "Alone … ", I would not follow it with an ellipsis, as if to tint my isolation with a note of melancholy that is not in my nature; nor with an exclamation mark: "Alone!", which would have had the pointless effect of appearing to challenge the world. I merely observe that I have grown up, lived, and am growing old alone.

It is loneliness that has forged my character, which is bad-tempered, and bronzed my soul, which is proud, and my body, which is sturdy.

My life is the story—and often the tragedy—of the solitary woman, her woes, her importance, the unequal and fascinating battle she has waged with herself, with men, and with the attractions, the weaknesses and the dangers that spring up everywhere.

Today, alone in the sunshine and snow … I shall continue, without husband, without children, without grandchildren, without all those delightful illusions, without all those delusions that make us believe that the world is inhabited by our other selves, to work and live 'alone'.

Coco en communiante

LITTLE COCO

E VERY CHILD HAS A SPECIAL PLACE, where he or She likes to hide, play and dream. Mine was an Auvergne cemetery. I knew no one there, not even the dead; I didn't grieve for anyone; no visitor ever came there. It was a little, old country cemetery, with neglected graves and overgrown grass. I was the queen of this secret garden. I loved its subterranean dwellers. "The dead are not dead as long as we think of them," I would tell myself. I became very fond of two unnamed tombs; these slabs of granite and basalt were my playroom, my boudoir, my den. I brought flowers there; on the humped mounds I devised hearts with cornflowers, stained-glass windows with poppies, citations with daisies. In between two mushroom-picking expeditions, I would bring my rag dolls on a visit, the ones I preferred to all the others because I had made them myself. I confided my joys and sorrows to my silent companions without disturbing their final rest.

I wanted to be sure that I was loved, but I lived with people who showed no pity. I like talking to myself and I don't listen to what I'm told: this is probably due to the fact that the first people to whom I opened my heart were the dead.

There we are arriving at my aunts' house, my father and I, at dusk. We are in deep mourning. My mother has just died. My two sisters have been sent to a convent. I, being the most sensible one, am entrusted to these aunts who are distant relations, my mother's first cousins. When we get there, we are greeted half-heartedly; they cut the wick of the lamp to see my face more clearly. My aunts have had supper; we haven't; they are surprised that people who have been travelling all day should not have eaten. This disturbs their routine and their household management, but eventually they overcome their harsh, provincial austerity and say reluctantly: "We shall cook you two boiled eggs." Little Coco can sense their reluctance and is offended; she is dying of hunger, but at the sight of the eggs she shakes her head, she refuses them, she declines, she states in a loud voice that she does not like eggs, she loathes them; in actual fact, she loves them, but after this first meeting, on this dismal night, she needs to say no to something, to say no passionately to everything she is presented with, to the aunts, to everything around her, to the new life. During the ten years that she will spend in the Mont-Dore, little Coco will dig herself ever more deeply into her first lie, her stubborn refusal, until at last the undisputed legend—the first legend, which will be followed by so many more!—is given credence: "little Coco doesn't like eggs". Henceforth, whenever I am about to consume a fine mouthful of flambéed omelette, hoping that this myth concerning me will be forgotten, I shall hear my aunts' caustic voices saying to me: "you know very well they are made of eggs". Thus does the myth kill the hero.

I say no to everything, because of a fierce—too fierce—love of life, because of a need to be loved, because everything about my aunts irritates and upsets me. Horrible aunts! Adorable aunts! They belonged to that peasant bourgeoisie that never sets foot in town, or in their village, unless driven there by bad weather, for the winter, but which never loses touch with the earth that feeds them. Horrible aunts for whom love is a luxury and childhood a sin. Adorable aunts whose chimney place overflows with salted and smoked meats, dressers with salted butter or jams, cupboards with fine Issoire linen sheets, which our Auvergne hawkers sell all over the world. There is so much linen-ware in their house that they need only send it to the laundry twice a year. I know that people from the Auvergne are not supposed to be very clean, but compared to our well-worn bundles nowadays, it was a great deal of linen. Our servants wear pleated head-dresses, because from the age of fifteen they have cut off and sold their hair; it's a custom that dates back to the Gauls; Roman women were already wearing our hair. I am sent to school and to catechism classes. I don't learn a thing there. My knowledge would never have anything to do with what the teachers taught me; the God I believe in would not be the god of the priests. My aunt makes me recite my lesson; since she has forgotten her catechism, she looks in my book for her questions; I answer perfectly, and all the better because I have discovered another catechism in the attic and have torn out the pages one by one, and so can hide the passages I am being questioned about in the palm of my hand.

The attic ... what resources there are in this attic! It's my library. I read everything. I find the fictional material there upon which my inner life will feed. We never bought books at home; we cut out the serial from the newspaper and we sewed together those long sheets of yellow paper. That's what little Coco lapped up in secret, in the so-called attic. I copied down whole passages from novels I had read, which I would slip into my homework: "Where on earth did you get hold of all that?" the teacher asked me. Those novels taught me about life; they nourished my sensibility and my pride. I have always been proud.

I hate to demean myself, to submit to anyone, to humiliate myself, not to speak plainly, to give in, not to have my own way. Now as then, pride is present in whatever I do, in my gestures, in the hardness of my voice, in my steely gaze, in my anxious and well-developed facial features, in my entire being. I am the only volcanic crater in the Auvergne that is not extinct.

My hair is still black, rather like a horse's mane, my eyebrows are as black as our chimney sweep's, my skin is dark like the lava from our mountains, and my character is as black as the core of a land that has never capitulated. I was a rebellious child, a rebellious lover, a rebellious fashion designer, a true Lucifer. My aunts were not wicked people, but I thought they were, which amounts to the same thing. The Mont-Dore was not really a terrible place, but it was for me, and it was what I endured at the time that has strengthened me; I owe my powerful build to my very tough upbringing. Yes, pride is the key to my bad temper, to my gypsy-like independence, to my antisocial nature; it is also the secret of my strength and my success; it's the Ariadne's thread that has always enabled me to find my way back.

For sometimes I lose myself. In the maze of my legendary fame, for example. Each of us has his or her legend, foolish and wonderful. Mine, to which Paris and the provinces, idiots and artists, poets and society people have contributed, is so varied, so complex, so straightforward and so complicated at the same time, that I lose myself within it. Not only does it disfigure me, but it reconstructs another aspect of me; when I want to recognise myself, all I have to do is think of that pride that is both my flaw and my virtue.

My legend is based upon two indestructible pillars: the first is that I have come up from goodness knows where; from the music hall, the opera or the brothel; I'm sorry, for that would have been more amusing; the second is that I am Queen Midas.

It was thought that I had a mind for business that I don't have. I am not Madame Curie, but nor am I Madame Hanau. Business matters and balance sheets bore me to death. If I want to add up, I count on my fingers.

It irritates me when I hear people say that I've been lucky. No one has worked harder than me. Those who dream up legends are lazy folk; if they weren't, they would go and investigate more deeply, instead of inventing things. The notion that anyone could construct what I have built up, without working, as if by magic, by rubbing Aladdin's lamp and simply making a wish, is nothing but pure imagination. (Pure … or impure.) What I say here will not change anything, in any case: nothing.

The legend has a harder life than the subject; reality is sad, and that handsome parasite that is the imagination will always be preferred to it. May my legend gain ground, I wish it a long and happy life! And many are the times that I shall continue to meet people who will talk to me about "Mlle C whom they know very well", without realising that it is her they are addressing.

"My earliest childhood". Those words, which are usually linked together, make me shudder. No childhood was less gentle. All too soon, I realised that life was a serious matter. My mother, who was already very ill, would take us, my two sisters and me, to the home of an elderly uncle (I was five years old) who was known as the "uncle from Issoire". We were shut away in a room covered in red wallpaper. To begin with, we were very well behaved; then we noticed that the red wallpaper was very damp and could be peeled off the wall, and we tore off a little strip to begin with; it was great fun. By pulling a little harder, a large section of wallpaper came away; it was extremely amusing; we climbed up on a chair; without any effort, all the paper came off … We piled up the chairs one on top of the other: the wall appeared with its pink plaster; how marvellous! We placed the stack of chairs on a table and managed to strip away the paper as far as the ceiling: the pleasure was sublime! At last, my mother came in; she stood stock still, contemplating the disaster. She didn't say a word to us; in the depths of her despair all she did was weep silently; no reprimand could have had such an effect on me; I ran away, howling with sorrow: we never saw the uncle from Issoire again.

Yes, life was a solemn affair, since it caused mothers to cry. On another occasion, my sisters and I were put to bed in a room, not normally occupied, in which bunches of grapes were hanging on a string from the ceiling. The grapes, in their paper bags, would keep in this way throughout the winter: I took a pillow, threw it in the air, and knocked down one bunch; another followed; then another; the grapes lay scattered on the ground; I hit them with the bolster, this way and that; soon the entire harvest was strewn over the wooden floor. For the first time in my life, I was whipped. The humiliation was something I would never forget.

"These people live like travelling circus folk," an aunt remarked.

"Coco will turn out badly," another replied.

"We'll have to sell her to the gypsies … "

"Stinging nettles … " (domestic chastisements only made me more uncivilised, more fractious).

When I observe how early happiness handicaps people, I do not regret having been deeply unhappy to begin with. You have to be a truly decent person to put up with a good education. I would not have had a different destiny to mine for anything in the world.

I was naughty, bad-tempered, thieving, hypocritical and eavesdropping. I only liked to eat what I had stolen. Unbeknown to my aunts, I would hide away and cut myself huge slices of bread; the cook used to say to me: "You'll cut yourself in half"; in order to be free, I took my bread to the lavatory. The proud know only one supreme good—freedom!

But to be free, one needs money. I thought of nothing but the money that opens the prison gate. The catalogues I read gave me wild dreams of spending. I imagined myself wearing a white woollen dress; I wanted a bedroom painted in white gloss, with white curtains. What a contrast this white made with the dark house in which my aunts confined me. Shortly before he left for America, my father brought me a first communion dress, in white chiffon, with a crown of roses. So as to punish me for being proud, my aunts said to me: "You're not going to wear your crown of roses, you'll wear a hat." What agony it was, on top of so many other things, such as the shame of having to confess to the priest that I had stolen two cherries! To be deprived of the crown! For me, the eldest, not to be able to wear it!

I threw my arms around my father's neck. "Take me away from here!" "Now, now, my dear Coco, everything will be all right, I'll be back, I'll take you with me, we'll have a home again … " Those were his last words. He didn't come back. I never lived under my father's roof again. He occasionally wrote and told me to trust him and said that his business was doing well. And then that was all—we never heard another word from him.

At the time, I often used to think about dying; the idea of causing a great fuss, of upsetting my aunts, of letting everyone know how wicked they were, fascinated me. I dreamt about setting fire to the barn. They kept on telling me that on my father's side I came from a family of nobodies. "You wouldn't hold your head so high if you knew that your grandmother was a shepherdess," they used to say. In which they were mistaken, for I found it delightful to have a granny with a crook, putting sheep adorned with ribbons out to graze. (Up until the day not long ago when, during the Occupation, I was with my aunt, Adrienne de Nexon, my grandparents' daughter, who was obliged to provide proof of her ancestry; we discovered that this shameful side of my family, in spite of the shepherdess, was better than the other side.)

I behaved properly in front of strangers. The local people used to say: "Little Coco has good manners". I was well brought up, like a dog that has been well trained. I kept my fits of madness to myself, except for one occasion when I slid down the banisters and landed in the middle of the drawing room, among the guests. If I was given a five-franc coin, I would squander it on presents. "You'll end up poor," my aunts kept on saying.

Another aunt of mine, my father's sister, who was much younger than the others and was beautiful, with long hair, would sometimes come to the house.

"We're going to take tea," I would say.

"Tea? Where have you heard about taking tea?" asked the other aunts.

"In the fashion magazines. In Paris, they take tea; whether you like it or not, that's what happens. There's a whole ceremony. You place the teapot beneath a 'cosy'; that's what it's called. You invite your friends; you serve them from an embroidered table mat."

"Coco, you're crazy!"

"I want tea."

"There isn't any."

"The chemist has some."

When I got my tea, my Aunt Adrienne said:
"Let's play at being ladies. Strong or weak?"
"I don't want to."
"Ladies don't say 'I don't want to'."
"What do you mean by ladies?"
"Those in 'aristocratic circles'."
"Who will take us there?"

We drained our cups. I ventured to ask my Aunt Adrienne:
"Apart from ladies, who goes to tea parties?"
"Elegant men, those who do nothing; they are far more handsome than those who work."
"Don't they do anything?"
"You should see them … They do lots of things."
"Adrienne, leave the child alone; you'll bewilder her."

My aunts owned some grazing land, for they had a little property; fields of close-cropped grass, which were poor for producing milk, but very much enjoyed by horses. They bred horses, in the most basic sort of way, which meant allowing the animals to graze freely. They sold their best products to the army (who, then, spoke about the infantry!). Untameable, like our chickens, I ran all over our farm buildings with the little peasant children. I mounted our horses bare-back (at sixteen, I had never seen a saddle), I caught hold of our best animals (or occasionally other people's, as I fancied) by their manes or their tails. I stole all the carrots from the house to feed them. How I loved it when the handsome soldiers did their rounds, and the visits of the cavalry officers who came to see our herd.

Fine hussars or chasseurs, with sky-blue dolmans and black frogging, and their pelisses on their shoulders. They came every year in their beautifully harnessed phaetons; they looked in the horses' mouths to see how old they were, stroked their fetlocks to check that they weren't inflamed, and slapped their flanks; it was a great party; a party that for me was fraught with a degree of anxiety: supposing they were going to take my favourite horses away from me? But they didn't choose them; they were careful not to, for I had made them gallop so much on hard and flinty ground while they were unshod and in the fields, that their feet had been affected. I can still see the officer coming into our house, after the inspection, and warming himself by the kitchen hearth: "These horses have hooves like cattle, their soles have gone and their frogs are rotten!" he said, referring to our best-looking creatures. I no longer dared to look the officer in the eye, but he had seen through me; as soon as my aunts had turned away, he whispered in a low voice: "So you've been galloping without shoes, eh, you little rascal?"

It's not that I love horses. I've never been like the 'horsey folk' who groom them and comb them for fun, or like the Englishwomen who, as soon as they have a spare moment, spend it in the stable.

Yet it is nevertheless true that horses have influenced the course of my life.

This is how—

It so happened that my aunts had sent me to spend the summer at Vichy, with my grandfather, who was taking the waters. I was so glad to have escaped from Mont-Dore, from the gloomy house, from needlework, from my trousseau; embroidering initials on the towels for my future household, and sewing crosses in Russian stitching on my nightdresses, for a hypothetical wedding night, made me feel ill; in a fury, I spat on my trousseau. I was sixteen. I was becoming pretty. I had a face that was as plump as a fist, hidden in a vast swathe of black hair that reached the ground. Vichy! How wonderful after Mont-Dore! I was no longer under the eye of my aunts; how much I preferred the patriarchal supervision of my grandparents! I walked outside on my own all day long, I strode out ahead of me, nose in the air. Away from my chestnut groves, Vichy was a fairyland. A ghastly fairyland in reality, but wonderful to fresh eyes. At last I could see at close hand those 'bathers' whom we did not dare look at behind Persian blinds in Thiers; we were forbidden to look at those 'eccentrics', the women who wore tartan dresses. In Vichy, I could satisfy my hunger. I found myself in the heart of the citadel of extravagance. Cosmopolitan society is like taking a journey without moving: Vichy was my first journey. Vichy would teach me about life. Young girls know everything today; as for us, we knew nothing, nothing, nothing. I don't regret it.

FROM COMPIÈGNE TO PAU

I N VICHY, I WATCHED THE LADIES—the old ladies—pass by, for there were only old people there. (In 1910, the young didn't drink alcohol and didn't look after their livers.) But I did not admit my disappointment. Everything enchanted me, even the engraved glasses used to drink water from the springs. Everywhere, 'foreign' was being spoken; foreign languages fascinated me; it was as if they were the passwords of a great secret society.

I watched the eccentric people parade past and I said to myself: "There exist in the world things that I should be and which I am not." I would become one of them, and much sooner than I thought. At a tea party I was taken to by my relatives, I made the acquaintance of a young man, M B; he owned a racing stable.

"How lucky you are," I said with naive enthusiasm, "to have racehorses!"

"Would you like to come to a training session, Mademoiselle?"

"What a dream!"

We arranged to meet the following day. After crossing the River Allier, beyond the footbridge, I went down into the fields and found myself in front of the horse boxes. There was a good smell of churned-up water; you could hear the roaring from the weir. A straight path, newly cut, stretched away, parallel to the river; sand, white railings and, in the background, the hills of the Bourbonnais. The sun glinted on the slopes of Ganat.

The jockeys and the stable lads followed one another, at a walk, their knees tucked under their chins.

"What a wonderful life," I sighed.

"It's mine all the year round," said M B. "I live in Compiègne. Why shouldn't it be yours too?"

I said yes. I would never see Mont-Dore again. I would never see my aunts again.

That is my childhood, the childhood of an orphan, retold by a girl who knew no home, no love, no father and mother. It was terrible, but I don't regret a thing. I have been ungrateful to the wicked aunts: I owe them everything, a rebellious child makes for a well-prepared and very strong human being. (Aged eleven, I had much more strength than I do now.)

It is kisses, hugs, teachers and vitamins that kill children and prepare them for being weak or unhappy. It is wicked aunts who make conquerors of them … And who develop inferiority complexes in them. In my case, this gave me the opposite: superiority complexes. Beneath maliciousness, there is strength; beneath pride, there is the taste for success and the love of importance. Children who have teachers learn. I was self-taught;

I learnt badly, haphazardly. And yet, when life put me in touch with those who were the most delightful or brilliant people of my age, a Stravinsky, or a Picasso, I neither felt stupid, nor embarrassed. Why?

Because I had worked out on my own that which cannot be taught. I will return to this frequently. For the time being, I want to end on this important aphorism, which is the secret of my success, and perhaps that of civilisation; confronted with ruthless techniques of doing things: *it's with what cannot be taught that one succeeds.*

I had run away. My grandfather believed I had returned home; my aunts thought I was at my grandfather's house. Someone would eventually realise that I was neither with the one nor the other.

I had followed M B and I was living in Compiègne. I was very bored. I was constantly weeping. I had told him a whole litany of lies about my miserable childhood. I had to disabuse him. I wept for an entire year. The only happy times were those I spent on horseback, in the forest. I learnt to ride, for up until then I hadn't the first idea about riding horses. I was never a horsewoman, but at that time I couldn't even ride side-saddle … The fairy tale was over. I was nothing but a lost child. I didn't dare write to anyone. M B was frightened of the police. His friends told him: "Coco is too young, send her back home." M B would have been delighted to see me go, but I had no home any more. M B had just broken off his relationship with a well-known beauty of the period, Émilienne d'Alençon; his house was full of photographs of her. "How lovely she is!" I said to him naively. "Could I meet her?" He shrugged his shoulders and replied that it was impossible. I didn't understand. M B was afraid of the police, and I was afraid of the servants. I had lied to M B. I had kept my age a secret, telling him that I was nearly twenty: in actual fact I was sixteen. I made an appearance at the Compiègne races. I wore a straw boater, set very low on the head, and a little country suit, and I followed events from the end of my lorgnette. I was convinced no one was taking any notice of me, which shows how little I knew about life in the provinces. In reality this ridiculous, badly dressed, shy little creature, with her three big plaits and a ribbon in her hair, intrigued everybody.

M B took me to Pau. The mild winters in the Basses-Pyrénées; the babbling mountain streams that flow down to the plains; the fields that are green in every season; the tall, grass-covered jumps, the red coats in the rain, and the best fox-hunting land in Europe …

In the distance I could see the old castle with its six towers and the snow-capped Pyrenees standing out against the blue sky. The saddle horses, the hunters, the half-breeds, the people from Tarbes who had been wandering around the Place Royale since morning. I can still hear the sound of hooves on the cobblestones.

In Pau I met an Englishman. We made each other's acquaintance when we were out horse-trekking one day; we all lived on horseback. The first person to take a tumble stood the others a glass of Jurançon. The wine was young, intoxicating and quite unusual. The young man was handsome, very tanned and attractive. More than handsome, he was magnificent. I admired his nonchalance, and his green eyes. He rode bold and very powerful horses. I fell in love with him. I had never loved M B. Not a word was exchanged between this Englishman and me. One day I heard that he was leaving Pau.

"You're going away?" I asked.

"Yes, unfortunately," he said.

"At what time?"

The following day, I was at the station. I climbed onto the train.

en 1912 Coco avait encore la masse noire
de ses cheveux longs

ARRIVAL IN PARIS

T HE NAME OF THE HANDSOME ENGLISHMAN was Boy Capel. He didn't know what to do with me either. He took me to Paris and set me up in a hotel. Young M B, who was very distressed, was packed off to Argentina by his family.

M B and Capel had taken pity on me; they thought of me as a poor, abandoned sparrow; in actual fact, I was a monster. I gradually learnt about life, I mean how to cope with it. I was highly intelligent, far more intelligent than I am now. I was unlike anyone else, either physically or mentally. I liked solitude; instinctively I loved what was beautiful and loathed prettiness. I always told the truth. I was very opinionated for my age. I could tell what was fake, conventional or bad. Paris made me feel dreadfully frightened. I didn't go out. I knew nothing about the world. I was unaware of social nuances, of family histories, the scandals, the allusions, all the things that Paris knew about and which are not written down anywhere, and since I was much too proud to ask questions, I remained in ignorance.

Boy Capel, a highly cultured man and an eccentric character, eventually came to understand me very well.

"She looks frivolous," he would say, "but she isn't."

He didn't want me to have friends. He added:

"They would damage you."

He is the only man I have loved. He is dead. I have never forgotten him. He was the great stroke of luck in my life; I had met a human being who did not demoralise me. He had a very strong and unusual character, and he was a passionate and single-minded sort of man; he shaped me, he knew how to develop what was unique in me, at the cost of everything else. At the age of thirty, at a time when young men fritter away their wealth, Boy Capel had already made his fortune in coal transportation. He owned a stable of polo ponies. He was one of the lions of London society. For me he was my father, my brother, my entire family. When war came, he knew how to win over old Clemenceau, who thought the world of him. His manners were refined, his social success was dazzling. He was only happy in the company of the little brute from the provinces, the unruly child who had followed him. We never went out together (at that time, Paris still had principles). We would delay the delights of advertising our love until later, when we were married. One day, however, on a whim, I insisted that Boy Capel should put off attending an important gala at the Casino in Deauville and dine there alone with me. All eyes were on us: my timid entrance, my awkwardness which contrasted with a wonderfully simple white dress, attracted people's attention. The beauties of the period, with that intuition women have for threats unknown, were alarmed; they forgot their lords and their maharajahs; Boy's place at their table remained empty. Pauline de Laborde and Marthe Letellier could not take their eyes off me. One of the elegant celebrities recalling that dinner to me, which I had forgotten, many years later, commented: "That evening you gave me one of the greatest shocks of my life." "How well I understand Boy deserting us for her," said an Englishwoman at that dinner party; her objectivity merely poured oil on the fire.

My success dates from that evening; to begin with it was an English success. I have always succeeded with the English, I don't know why. Relationships between England and France have been through many trials, but my English friends have always remained loyal to me. One of them confessed to me, not long ago: "Since I've known you, I've come to like France again."

Boy Capel's beautiful girlfriends would say to him angrily: "Drop that woman." Not being in the least jealous, I pushed him into their arms; this baffled them and they kept on repeating: "Drop that woman". He replied in that utterly natural way he had, one that astonished people in an age of poseurs: "No. You might as well ask me to chop off a leg." He needed me.

M B returned from Argentina. He brought me some lemons, rotten ones what's more, in a bag.

"How are you getting on with your Englishman?"

"I'm getting on … as men and women do."

"That's perfect. Continue."

This simple bit of dialogue conveys badly what was an extremely complicated situation. Today everything is easy. Speed governs affairs of the heart, as it does everything else. But before the situation was resolved, there were tears and quarrels. Boy was English, he didn't understand; everything became muddled. He was very moral. I distanced him from his friends, who loathed me. They lived with tarts. Boy hid me away; he wouldn't allow me to go around with them. I asked him why.

"The girls are so pretty," I said.

"Yes, but nothing else."

"Why do they never come to the house?"

"Because ... you're not one of them, you're not like anyone else. And then because, when we are married ... "

"Me, I'm not pretty ... "

"Of course you're not pretty, but I have nothing more beautiful than you."

Our house was full of flowers, but beneath the luxurious surroundings Boy Capel maintained a strict outlook, in keeping with his moral character, which was that of the well-brought-up Englishman. In educating me, he did not spare me; he commented on my conduct: "You behaved badly ... you lied ... you were wrong." He had that gently authoritative manner of men who know women well, and who love them implicitly.

One day, I said to Boy Capel:

"I'm going to work. I want to make hats."

"Fine. You'll do very well. You'll get though a lot of money, but that doesn't matter, you need to keep busy, it's an excellent idea. The most important thing is that you're happy."

The women I saw at the races wore enormous loaves on their heads, constructions made of feathers and improved with fruits and plumes; but worst of all, which appalled me, their hats did not fit on their heads. (I have mentioned that I wore mine pulled down over the ears.)

I rented rooms on the first floor of a building in the rue Cambon. I still have it. On the door, it read: '*Chanel, modes*'. Capel put an excellent woman at my disposal, Madame Aubert, whose real name was Mademoiselle de Saint-Pons. She advised me and guided me. In the grandstands, people began talking about my amazing, unusual hats, so neat and austere, which were somehow a foretaste of the iron age that was to come, but which had not yet dawned. Customers came, initially prompted by curiosity. One day I had a visit from one such woman, who admitted quite openly:

"I came … to have a look at you."

I was the curious creature, the little woman whose straw boater fitted her head, and whose head fitted her shoulders.

The more people came to call on me, the more I hid away. This habit has always remained with me. I never appeared at shows. One had to make conversation, which terrified me. And I didn't know how to sell; I've never known how to sell. When a customer insisted on seeing me, I went and hid in a cupboard.

"You go, Angèle."

"But it's you they want to see, Mademoiselle."

I wanted the earth to swallow me up. I thought that everybody was very intelligent and that I was stupid.

"But where is this little woman I've heard so much about?" the customer persisted.

"Do come, Mademoiselle!" begged Angèle.

"I can't. If they find the hat's too expensive, I feel I might give it away."

I had a premonition of this axiom, observed a thousand times since: "Every customer seen is a customer lost". If somebody encountered me accidentally in the shop, then I spoke, I prattled away, out of shyness; escaping through chit-chat: how many windbags, mocked for their self-assurance, are simply quiet people who, deep down, are frightened of silence.

I was extremely naive. I didn't begin to imagine that I was of interest to people; I didn't realise that it was me they were looking at. I thought of myself merely as a country girl, like so many others. The age of extravagant dresses, those dresses worn by heroines that I had dreamt about, was past. I had never even had those convent uniforms, with capes, adorned with pale blue Holy Ghost, or Children of Mary, ribbons, which are a child's pride and joy; I no longer thought about lace; I knew that extravagant things didn't suit me. All I kept were my goat-skin coat and my simple outfits.

"Since you are so attached to them," Capel said to me, "I'm going to get you to have the clothes you have always worn remade *elegantly*, by an English tailor."

Everything to do with rue Cambon stemmed from there.

Boy Capel had given me the wherewithal to have fun; I had so much fun that I forgot about love. In reality, he wanted to give me all the joie de vivre that he would forego.

"Tell me who you're sleeping with, it would amuse me greatly," I would say to him. (I don't know what word I used at the time, but not 'sleep'. In 1913 people didn't say that.)

He laughed:

"Do you think that makes my life easy? It complicates it. But then (and you don't appear to have any doubt about it), you're a woman."

Coco dans son salon bibliothèque de la rue Cambon

RUE CAMBON

IN THE AUVERGNE, throughout my childhood, my aunts had kept on telling me: "You won't have any money … you'll be very lucky if a farmer wants you". Very young, I had realised that without money you are nothing, that with money you can do anything. Or else, you had to depend on a husband. Without money, I would be forced to sit on my behind and wait for a gentleman to come and find me. And if you don't like him? The other girls resigned themselves, I didn't. I suffered in my pride. It was hellish. And I would say to myself over and over: money is the key to freedom. These reflections are self-evident; what gives them substance is that I discovered their reality at the age of twelve.

To begin with, you long for money. Then you develop a liking for work. Work has a much stronger flavour than money. Ultimately, money is nothing more than the symbol of independence. In my case, it only interested me because it flattered my pride. It wasn't a question of buying things, I've never wanted anything, just affection, and I had to buy my freedom and pay for it whatever the cost.

When I moved into the rue Cambon, I knew nothing about business matters, I didn't know what a bank or a cheque was. I was ashamed that I knew so little about life, but Boy Capel wanted me to remain the unsophisticated, untainted creature that he had discovered. "Business is a matter for banks", that was the only reply I was given. To enable me to start up, Capel had deposited securities as a guarantee with Lloyd's Bank, where he was a partner.

One evening, he took me to dinner in Saint-Germain.

"I'm making a lot of money," I told him immodestly, along the way. "Business is wonderful. It's very easy, all I have to do is draw cheques."

I had no idea at the time about what was meant by cost prices, accounting, etc. Rue Cambon was run chaotically.

All I bothered about was the shape of the hats, along with the childish pleasure of hearing myself called "Mademoiselle".

"Yes. That's very good. But you're in debt to the bank," my companion replied.

"What? In debt to the bank? But since I'm making money? If I weren't making any, the bank wouldn't give me any."

Capel began to laugh, somewhat sarcastically.

"The bank gives you money because I have deposited securities as a guarantee."

My heart started to thump.

"Do you mean to say that I haven't earned the money I spend? That money is mine!"

"No. It belongs to the bank."

I could feel the anger and despair rising. Once we had reached Saint-Germain, I carried on walking, walking straight ahead until I was exhausted.

"Only yesterday, the bank telephoned me … to say that you were withdrawing a little too much, my darling, but it's of no importance … "

"The bank rang *you*? And why not me? So I'm dependent on you?"

I felt sick. Impossible to eat. I insisted on going back to Paris. We went up to our flat in the avenue Gabriel. I glanced at the pretty things I had bought with what I thought were my profits. So all that had been paid for by him! I was living off him! There was thunder in the air that evening, but the storm within me was rumbling much louder. I began to hate this well-brought-up man who was paying for me. I threw my handbag straight at his face and I fled.

"Coco! … You're crazy … " said Capel as he followed me.

I walked through the pouring rain, not knowing where I was going.

"Coco … Be reasonable."

He ran after me and caught up with me on the corner of the rue Cambon. We were both drenched. I was sobbing.

Capel took me home. The storm had stopped. The deep wound made in my pride was hurting me less. We had a very late supper … What a day! The following day, at first light, I was at rue Cambon.

"Angèle," I said to my head seamstress, "I am not here to have fun, or to spend money like water. I am here to make a fortune. From now on, no one will incur a centime without my permission."

"You're proud," Capel said to me. "You'll suffer … "

One year later, Capel's guarantee had become unnecessary; he could withdraw his securities; the profits from rue Cambon were enough for everything. Pride is a good thing, but that day my irresponsible youth came to an end.

A memory should have a moral ending: it's its raison d'être, otherwise it's mere gossip. It's through work that one achieves. Manna didn't fall on me from heaven; I moulded it with my own hands, in order to feed myself. "Everything Coco touches, she transforms into gold", my friends say. The secret of this success is that I have worked terribly hard. I have worked for fifty years, as much and more than anyone. Nothing can replace work, not securities, or nerve, or luck.

One day I ran into M B.

"Apparently you're working?" he said to me ironically. "Can't Capel support you then?"

What a joy it is to be able to respond to these idle rich, these petty horse-breeders: "I owe nothing to anybody"! I was my own master, and I depended on myself alone. Boy Capel was well aware that he didn't control me:

"I thought I'd given you a plaything, I gave you freedom," he once said to me in a melancholy voice.

1914. The war. Capel persuaded me to withdraw to Deauville where he rented a villa for his ponies. Many elegant ladies had come to Deauville. Not only did they need to have hats made for them, but soon, because there were no dressmakers, they had to be properly attired. I only had milliners with me; I converted them into dressmakers. There was a shortage of material. I cut jerseys for them from the sweaters the stable lads wore and from the knitted training garments that I wore myself. By the end of the first summer of the war, I had earned two hundred thousand gold francs, and ... the stable had ousted the enclosure into second place!

What did I know about my new profession? Nothing. I didn't know dressmakers existed. Did I have any idea of the revolution that I was about to stir up in clothing? By no means. One world was ending, another was about to be born. I was in the right place; an opportunity beckoned, I took it. I had grown up with this new century: I was therefore the one to be consulted about its sartorial style. What were needed were simplicity, comfort and neatness: unwittingly, I offered all of that. True success is inevitable.

The enclosure before 1914! When I went to the races, I would never have thought that I was witnessing the death of luxury, the passing of the nineteenth century, the end of an era. An age of magnificence, but of decadence, the last reflections of a baroque style in which the ornate had killed off the figure, in which over-embellishment had stifled the body's architecture, just as parasites smother trees in tropical forests. Woman was no more than a pretext for riches, for lace, for sable, for chinchilla, for materials that were too precious. Complicated patterns, an excess of lace, of embroidery, of gauze, of flounces and over-layers had transformed what women wore into a monument of belated and flamboyant art. The trains of dresses swept up the dust, all the pastel shades reflected every colour in the rainbow in a thousand tints with a subtlety that faded into insipidness. There were parasols, aviaries and greenhouses in gardens. The uncommon had become the normal; wealth was as ordinary as poverty.

As a child, I had succumbed, like everyone else. In Mont-Dore, aged fifteen, I had been allowed to order a dress of my choice: my dress was mauve, as mauve as a bad novel published by Lemerre, laced at the back, as though I had had hundreds of maids, and with bunches of artificial Parma violets on each side, as in a play by Rostand; a collar held up by two stays that dug into my neck; below, at the back, a sweeping train with which to gather up all the sweethearts behind you.

I had one obsession when I ordered this dress—to look like the "lady with the metal hand". She was a woman from the neighbourhood. She was poor and spoke very little (in my region people say very little), and, prompted by some repressed narcissism, or secret day-dreaming, she dressed herself in some extraordinary clothes. She wore close-fitting dresses that filled me with admiration; but what left me open-mouthed was the fact that she had a mechanical hand, a kind of metal pincers in the shape of a hand, to hold her train and to raise it, like the tie-back of a curtain. She said modestly that she wore it to save money, but I saw it as the height of elegance. I would never dare to borrow this mechanical hand, which looked like a contraption for picking asparagus, but I promised myself a train like hers. Mine was so long that I carried it under my arm; how smart I was! I would go to mass dressed like this; I, too, would rustle and swish; I would amaze everybody … I got dressed, I went downstairs. The outcome was what one might expect: "And now," my aunts said, "go upstairs and get dressed for mass." It was a dreadful put-down! I cried during the service; I asked God to let me die.

This first failure was also my first lesson in tact and good taste provided by the provinces. Indirectly, it was my Auvergne aunts who imposed their modesty on the beautiful Parisian ladies. Years have gone by, and it is only now that I realise that the austerity of dark shades, the respect for colours borrowed from nature, the almost monastic cut of my summer alpaca wear and of my winter tweed suits, all that puritanism that elegant ladies would go crazy for, came from Mont-Dore. If I wore hats pulled down over my head, it is because the wind in the Auvergne might mess up my hair. I was a Quaker woman who was conquering Paris, just as the stiff Genevese or American cowl had conquered Versailles a hundred and fifty years previously.

1914 was still 1900, and 1900 was still the Second Empire, with its frenzy of easy money, its habits of straying from one style to another, of romantically taking its inspiration from every country and all periods, for it lacked a way of expressing itself honestly, and aesthetically pleasing appearance is never anything but the outer expression of moral honesty, of authentic feelings.

That is why I was born, that is why I have endured, that is why the outfit I wore at the races in 1913 can still be worn in 1946, because the new social conditions are still those that led me to clothe them.

That is why the rue Cambon has been the centre of good taste for thirty years. I had rediscovered honesty, and, in my own way, I made fashion honest.

In 1914, there were no sports dresses. Women attended sporting occasions rather as fifteenth-century ladies in conical hats attended tournaments. They wore very low girdles, and they were bound at the hips, legs, everywhere … Since they ate a great deal, they were stout, and since they were stout and didn't want to be, they strapped themselves in. The corset pushed the fat up to the bosom and hid it beneath the dress. By inventing the jersey, I liberated the body, I discarded the waist (and only reverted to it in 1930), I created a new shape; in order to conform to it all my customers, with the help of the war, became slim, "slim like Coco". Women came to me to buy their slim figures. "With Coco, you're young, do as she does," they would say to their suppliers. To the great indignation of couturiers, I shortened dresses. The jersey in those days was only worn underneath; I gave it the honour of being worn on top.

In 1917 I slashed my thick hair; to begin with I trimmed it bit by bit. Finally, I wore it short.

"Why have you cut your hair?"

"Because it annoys me."

And everyone went into raptures, saying that I looked like "a young boy, a little shepherd". (That was beginning to become a compliment, for a woman.)

I had decided to replace expensive furs with the humblest hides. Chinchilla no longer arrived from South America, or sable from the Russia of the czars. I used rabbit. In this way, I made poor people and small retailers wealthy; the large stores have never forgiven me.

"Coco succeeds because there are no more grand soirées," said the best known couturiers of the pre-1914 years, "but an evening dress ... "

An evening dress, it's the easiest thing. The jersey is another matter! Like Lycurgus, I disapproved of expensive materials. A fine fabric is beautiful in itself, but the more lavish a dress is, the poorer it becomes. People confused poverty with simplicity. (It's better, by the way, to deprive yourself of things than for others to do so.)

After 1920, the great couturiers tried to fight back. At about that time, I remember contemplating the auditorium at the Opéra from the back of a box. All those gaudy, resuscitated colours shocked me; those reds, those greens, those electric blues, the entire Rimsky-Korsakov and Gustave Moreau palette, brought back into fashion by Paul Poiret, made me feel ill. The Ballets Russes were stage décor, not couture. I remember only too well saying to someone sitting beside me:

"These colours are impossible. These women, I'm bloody well going to dress them in black."

So I imposed black; it's still going strong today, for black wipes out everything else around. I used to tolerate colours, but I treated them as monochrome masses. The French don't have a sense of blocks of colour; what makes a herbaceous border beautiful in an English garden is the massed array; a begonia, a marguerite, a larkspur ... on their own, they're not at all special, but over a space twenty feet thick, the accumulation of flowers becomes magnificent.

"This removes all originality from a woman!"
Wrong: women retain their individual beauty by belonging to
an ensemble. Take a bit-part actress in a music hall; isolate her,
and she's a ghastly puppet; put her back in the chorus line, and
not only does she resume all her characteristics, but, compared
to those alongside her, her personality is released.

I brought in tweeds from Scotland; home-spuns came to oust
crepes and muslins. I arranged for woollens to be washed less,
so that they kept their softness; in France we wash too much. I
asked wholesalers for natural colours; I wanted women to be
guided by nature, to obey the mimicry of animals. A green dress
on a lawn is perfectly acceptable. I called on Rodier: he proudly
showed me a range of twenty-five different greys. How could
a customer reach a decision? She would rely on her husband,
who had other things to do, the woman would postpone her
order, and the sales people wasted their time; once the dress was
cut, she would change her mind etc. I really had to congratulate
myself for having simplified the choice.

Let's stop there. I'm not chattering on to expound truths that
have become truisms. All this is common knowledge, and we
have moved on. For a quarter-of-a-century, the fashion pages
and the magazines have been full of my working methods: how
I work with the mannequins themselves, whereas the others
make drawings, or construct dolls or models. (My scissors are not
those of Praxiteles, but nonetheless, I sculpt my pattern more
than I draw it.) Why are my mannequins always the same, to
such an extent that their faces and bodies are more familiar to

me than my own? Why is it that everything that comes from my workshops, from the simplest suit to the smartest dress, appears to be cut by the same hand?

Were I writing a technical handbook, I would say to you: "A well-made dress suits everyone." Having said that, no woman has the same arm width; the shape of the shoulder is never the same ... everything depends on the shoulder; if a dress doesn't fit on the shoulder, it will never fit ... The front doesn't move, it's the back that takes the strain. A plump woman always has a narrow back, a slim woman always has a wide back; the back must have room to move, at least ten centimetres; you have to be able to bend down, play golf, put on your shoes. The customer's measurements must therefore be taken with the arms crossed ...

All the articulation of the body is in the back; *all movements stem from the back*; so one has to insert as much material there as possible ... A garment must move over the body; a garment should be fitted when one is standing still, and be too big when one moves. No one should be frightened of pleats: a pleat is always beautiful if it is useful ... Not all women are Venus; however, nothing should be concealed, trying to cover up something only accentuates it ... You don't get rid of bad legs by lengthening a dress ... With the mannequin, I think firstly of the clothed shape; the choice of material can come later; cloth that is well-fitted is prettier than anything ... The art of couture lies in knowing how to enhance: raising the waist in front to make the woman appear taller; lowering the back to avoid sagging bottoms (the 'pear-shaped' bottom is, alas, all too frequent!). The dress must be cut longer at the back because it rides up. Everything that makes the neck longer is attractive ...

I could go on like this for hours and hours: it would only be of interest to a few people, these basic facts are well known to all the specialists anyway, and thousands of copies of *Marie-Claire* have circulated them to the humblest dwellings; as to America, I am amazed to see, when I go there, that they know it all: the year in which I began making long dresses, and which year I shortened them. I don't have to explain my creations; they have explained themselves.

There, in a word, is why I would never tell you how a dress is made: I have never been a dressmaker. I admire those who can sew enormously: I have never known how; I prick my fingers; in any case, everybody knows how to make dresses nowadays. Gorgeous gentlemen who have failed at the Ecole Polytechnique know how to make them. Doddery old ladies know how to make them; they have used a needle all their lives; they are eminently sympathetic people.

Me, I am quite the opposite. I am a loathsome person and I hope that these sincere remarks will be appreciated.

Boy Capel and I lived in the Avenue Gabriel, in a delightful apartment. The first time I saw a coromandel screen, I exclaimed:
  "How beautiful it is!"

I had never said that about any object.

"You who are such an artistic person … " an elderly gentleman whom I didn't know said to me at a dinner party.

"I am not an artistic person."

"Then," he replied, squinting anxiously at my invitation card, "you are not Mlle Chanel."

"No, I am not her," I replied, to simplify things.

I have had twenty-one coromandel screens. They play the role that tapestries did in the Middle Ages; they allow you to recreate your home everywhere. Bérard used to say to me:

"You're the most eccentric person on earth."

But Cocteau, who knew me better, said:

"I don't dare tell people how you live, rising at seven o'clock, always in bed by nine, no one would ever believe it. And you don't care about a thing!"

I don't like eccentricity except in others.

I had the first carpets dyed beige. It reminded me of the soil. All the furnishings immediately became beige. Until the day came when the interior designers begged for mercy.

"Try white satin," I told them.

"What a good idea!"

And their designs were shrouded in snow, just as Mrs Somerset Maugham's shop in London became buried in naive innocence and white satin. Lacquerware, Chinese blues and whites, expensively designed rice papers, English silverware, white flowers in vases.

I have never forgotten how astonished Henry Bernstein was the first time he came to avenue Gabriel:

"How lovely it is here!"

(Since then, Antoinette Bernstein's delicate hand has put on the market this new decorative art which, from the Gymnase theatre to the Ambassadeurs, has made its way to all levels of society.)

Eccentricity was dying out; I hope, what's more, that I helped kill it off. Paul Poiret, a most inventive couturier, dressed women in costumes. The most intimate lunch party became a Chabrillan[2] ball, the most modest tea party looked like something from the Baghdad of the Caliphs. The last courtesans, admirable creatures, who have done so much for the glory of our arts, Canada, Forsane, Marie-Louise Herouet, Madame Iribe, would come by, to the sound of the tango, wearing bell-shaped dresses, with greyhounds and cheetahs at their side.

It was delightful, but easy. (A Scheherazade is very easy, a little black dress is very difficult.) One must beware of originality; in dressmaking, you immediately descend to disguise and decoration, you lapse into stage design. This princess, who is so happy with her green scarf printed in all the signs of the zodiac, will only astonish those who don't know; as paradoxical as it may seem, it has to be said that extravagance kills the personality. All the superlatives are devalued. An American delighted me with this compliment:

"To have spent so much money without it showing!"

---

2   Named after a celebrated nineteenth-century courtesan. [Tr]

Most of all, I bought books—to read them. Books have been my best friends. Just as the radio is a box full of lies, so each book is a treasure. The very worst book has something to say to you, something truthful. The silliest books are masterpieces of human experience. I have come across many very intelligent and highly cultivated people; they were astonished by what I knew; they would have been much more so if I had told them that I had learnt about life through novels. If I had daughters, I would give them novels for their instruction. There you find all the great unwritten laws that govern mankind. In my region of the country people didn't speak; they were not taught through the oral tradition. From the serial novels, read in the barn by the light of a candle stolen from the maid, to the greatest classics, all novels are reality in the guise of dreams. As a child, I instinctively read catalogues like novels—novels are merely big catalogues.

"I never give you presents," Boy Capel said to me.

"That's true."

The following day I opened the casket he sent me: it contained a tiara. I had never seen a tiara. I didn't know where to put it. Should I wear it round my neck? Angèle said to me: "You wear it on your head; it's for the Opera."

I wanted to go to the Opera, in the way a child demands to go to a show at the Châtelet theatre. I also discovered that men sent flowers.

"You could send me flowers," I said to Capel.

Half-an-hour later, I received a bouquet. I was delighted. Half-an-hour later, a second bouquet. I was pleased. Half-an-hour later, another bouquet. This was becoming monotonous.

Every half-hour the bouquets kept arriving in this way for two days. Boy Capel wanted to train me. I understood the lesson. He trained me for happiness.

Thus did our happy days pass at avenue Gabriel. I hardly ever went out. I dressed in the evening to please Capel, knowing very well that there would shortly be a moment when he would say: "why go out, after all, we're very comfortable here". He liked me among my surroundings, and there's a girl-from-the-harem side of me which suited this seclusion very well.

The outside world seemed unreal to me; I never got into the habit of moving about in it; like children, I had no sense of social perspective; the mental picture I had of Paris resembled a fifteenth-century panel in its unworldliness. One day, for example, I went to the Chambre; I was in the diplomatic gallery, in the seats reserved for the British Embassy. A young speaker was attacking Clemenceau in a cutting, sarcastic and extremely discourteous tone of voice. My reactions were those of the denizens of the gods faced with this treacherous tirade; I shouted out in a loud voice: "Shame on you, insulting the saviour of the nation!" A commotion, everyone glared at me, the usher stormed up, etc.

Capel brought to Clemenceau's home, where he was always welcome, the mindset of a businessman who was not hampered either by precedents or hierarchy. He provided simple solutions and good practical advice, which was not always followed. Clemenceau took a fancy to him, in the way that old men do when they are in a hurry; he could not do without him, and he begged him to accept the job of military attaché, which he could arrange quite easily with the British government. Capel, who did not want to fall out with Spears, refused.

When peace came (in those days peace came after war), Capel was killed in a motor accident. I shall not embellish this memory … His death was a terrible blow to me. In losing Capel, I lost everything. "He was much too good to remain among us," wrote Clemenceau. Boy was a rare spirit, an unusual character, a young man who had the experience of a fifty-year-old, a gentle, playful authority, and an ironic severity that charmed people and won them over. Beneath his dandyism, he was very serious, far more cultured than the polo players and big businessmen, with a deep inner life that extended to magical and theosophical levels. He wrote a great deal, without ever publishing anything; writings that were often prophetic; he had foreseen that the 1914 war was only the prelude to another great conflict that would be far more dreadful. He left a void in me that the years have not filled. I had the impression that, from the beyond, he was continuing to protect me … One day, in Paris, I had a visit from an unknown Hindu gentleman.

"I have a message for you, Mademoiselle. A message from someone you know … This person is living in a place of happiness, in a world where nothing can trouble him any longer. Receive this message of which I am the bearer, and whose meaning you will certainly understand."

And the Hindu man passed on the mysterious message; it was a secret that no one, other than Capel and I, could have known.

What followed was not a life of happiness, I have to say, however surprising it may seem. What kind of person was I then? After days spent working at rue Cambon, all I thought of was staying at home, similar in that respect to many busy Parisians, too busy to go out in the evening. (That is something that surprises people from the countryside, foreigners, and Americans especially: many French people do not live in the street or in cafés; they live at home.)

If I have known how to make the people around me happy, I don't have a sense of happiness myself. Scandal upsets me. I am reticent in various ways. Just as I don't care to leave my home, I don't like being interrupted, I don't like changing my ideas. I loathe people putting order into my disorder, or into my mind. Order is a subjective phenomenon. I also loathe advice, not because I am stubborn, but, on the contrary, because I am easily influenced. Besides, people only offer you playthings, medicaments and advice that work for them. Neither do I like to attach myself to anyone, for as soon as I grow fond of someone, I become cowardly (it's my way of being good); and cowardice offends me. As Colette, in the words of Sido, says so profoundly: "Love is not an honourable sentiment". I love to criticise; the day I can no longer criticise, life will be over for me.

Others have lived out their youth. Mine was a dream. Reality would no doubt have been better. But I thrive on solitude. I stop winning the game as soon as a gentleman comes up to me and whispers in my ear:
"May I put a thousand francs behind you?"
In that case, I know I have lost beforehand.

I hate people touching me, rather as cats do. I walk straight along the path I have plotted for myself, even when it bores me; I am its slave, because I have chosen it freely. Being as tough as steel, I have never missed a day's work, and I've never been ill; I avoided various famous doctors who forecast different deadly diseases that I have failed to treat. Since the age of thirteen, I have no longer contemplated suicide.

I have made dresses. I could easily have done something else. It was an accident. I didn't like dresses, but I liked work. I have sacrificed everything to it, even love. Work has consumed my life.

Gradually, rather than be surrounded with friends, I have found it more convenient to surround myself with regular visitors to whom I can freely say: "go away now".

I gave my time to work alone. M A, whom I had offended, said to me one day:

"You dislike me."

I replied:

"When did you think I had the time to do that?"

For people think of everything, they imagine every sort of hypothesis, apart from one—that one works and that one takes no notice of them.

JOURNEY TO ITALY

I T WAS SHORTLY AFTER the death of Boy Capel that I made the acquaintance of the Sert household; that is to say of Misia, née Godebska, who was Polish, and José Maria Sert, who was Catalan. We were like new toys for each other ... The Serts were moved to see a young woman weeping her heart out in grief. They were in Italy; they decided against going to Venice, which was their fiefdom, where I did not wish to go, altered their itinerary for me, and took me off in a motor car.

So began a close relationship which would last until Sert's death, with all the ripples that a clash of characters as entrenched as ours can stir up. I shall try to describe, in the course of this memoir, the tortuous bends, or more precisely the zig-zags, for there were plenty of right angles, that this relationship took.

One day I went to ask St Anthony of Padua to help me to stop mourning. I can still see myself in the church, before the statue of the saint, to the left, among the fine sarcophagi of Venetian admirals. A man in front of me was resting his forehead against the stone slab; he had such a sad and beautiful face, there was so much rigidity and pain in him, and his exhausted head touched the ground with such weariness that a miracle took place within me. I'm a wretch, I told myself; how shameful! How could I dare compare my sorrow of a lost child, for whom life has scarcely begun, with someone in this distress?

An energy immediately flowed through me. I took new heart and decided to live.

'Môsieur' Sert was a personality, a character, much larger than in the painting of him. He was as munificent and immoral as a Renaissance man. He loved money, even though he was profligate. "You have to admit that Sert makes everything else seem rather drab," Misia said to me; it was true. He was the ideal travelling companion; always good-humoured, a cicerone of weird and prodigious erudition. Each tiny bit of knowledge was balanced by another, as were his spectacular pictorial fantasies. This huge, hairy monkey, with his tinted beard, his humped back, his enormous tortoiseshell spectacles—veritable wheels—loved everything colossal. He slept in black pyjamas, never washed, and, even naked, looked as though he was wearing a fur coat, so hirsute was he; it was just as indecent. He had hair everywhere, except on his head. He guided me through museums like a faun through a familiar forest, he explained everything to my attentive ignorance, he liked to educate me, and he found in me a naturalness that he preferred to all his erudition. We would make huge detours of a hundred kilometres in search of some *osteria* where you could eat birds rolled in vine leaves; from Ucellos to *ucelli*; Sert, who once upon a time had roamed around Italy on foot, by donkey, in every way imaginable, maintained that he remembered the place very well. He unfolded his maps. In the end, the restaurant was nowhere to be found.

"Toche" (that's what he called Misia), "we've made a mistake; we should have turned right. Let's go back!"

We got lost again. Then we bought a pig, which we took with us in the car and had roasted by the side of the road.

He was delighted by his mistakes. He revelled in the unforeseen. Very sober, and flanked by two women who ate very little, Sert, who was lavish by nature, ordered rare wines, and meals that made our table look like a painting by Veronese or Parmigiano. In his inside pocket Sert carried crumpled thousand-franc banknotes. What he did with the money has always been a mystery to me; I never saw him use it. And it was impossible to pay the tip:

"This dinner is mine, Madmachelle!" he said with his Spanish pronunciation which, through his beard, transformed the French language into an incomprehensible mish-mash.

"Don't order anything else, I shan't eat it, Monsieur."

"You won't eat it, but I shall order another three zabagliones with maraschino cherries! Whether you want it or not!"

'Jojo' knew about everything, the catalogue of Boltraffio's paintings, the travels of Antonello da Messina, the lives of the Saints, which Dürer had engraved at the age of fourteen, the prices which the 'hundred florins' with margins made of China paper had raised at the sale of the Hibbert collection, the art of backing and relining, which varnishes Annibale Caracci used; he could hold forth for hours on Tintoretto's use of madder lacquer.

Slyly, he would put down advance payments on any object that he was passionate about and which he wanted to prevent me buying. His motor car was packed with suitcases, canvases, Capodimonte porcelain, oranges, eighteenth-century Italian illustrated books and miniature cribs.

I travelled with both the Sert households (firstly, with Misia, then, after his divorce, with Russy Mdivani); two consecutive and very different wives; but Jojo—or Maidi, a simian nickname that Russy gave him—was always a wonderful companion. Sert was not a dandy; he was not interested in gossip; he lived so that he could express a personality that his monumental, colossal, colourful rococo paintings were not entirely able to do. He only liked things on a vast scale, kilometres of frescoes, palaces that could be assaulted by a busy, frivolous paintbrush; he was very eager for commissions, extremely clever at soliciting them, and he would begin again three times, as he did at Vich, working on a cathedral whose decorations failed to satisfy him. He threw himself at life with a voraciousness that did not exclude subtlety.

We arrived in Rome, weary and drained, and we were obliged to visit the city, by moonlight, until we were exhausted. At the Colosseum, he remembered the recollections of Thomas de Quincey, and he said some wonderful things about architecture, and about the parties that might still be given among these ruins.

"I can see it decorated with balloons painted in gold, Madmachelle, something light and floating to contrast with the severity of the architecture … Architecture is the skeleton of the city.

Everything is in the skeleton, Madmachelle; a face without bones doesn't last: you, for example, Madmachelle, you would make a very beautiful corpse ... "[3]

Sert was an enormous gnome who, inside his hump, like a magic sack, carried gold as well as rubbish, extremely poor taste and exquisite judgement, the priceless and the disgusting, diamonds and crap, kindness and sadism (Cocteau claimed that he cut off stork's beaks), the pros and the cons ("Sert yes, Sert no," Cocteau again used to say). Virtues and vices on a staggering scale. I remember that with Sert we used to play at "what-shall-we-buy-if-we win-the-jackpot"; and Sert, who loved the impossible, would say:
"I would commission a miniature ... from Sert."

It was impossible, too, to talk to 'Môsieur' Sert about his painting. These gigantic constructions, the hard work of his assistants (for he insisted, in person, on being faithful to his maquettes), the excessive use of silver and gold that failed to conceal a basic deficiency, those streams of redcurrant jam, those swollen muscles, those demented contortions of figures, those riotous shapes, left me feeling confused, and praise stuck in my throat.
"I can sense that you loathe that," Misia whispered to me, "but don't let him notice."
"Madmachelle, Picasso doesn't know how to draw ... don't drink this Orvieto wine, it only costs three liras ... Stick with this

---

3   In the original French, Coco Chanel takes great pleasure in affectionately mocking Sert's accent (*"Je vois"*, for example, becomes *"Che voà"*; *"architecture"* is written as *"ârchitechtûre"*, etc.) For her, too, he was always *"Môsieur Sert"*. [Tr]

Château-Yquem 1893; smell the sap, the bouquet! The lords of Yquem (who included Montaigne among their forebears) sold the vineyard in 1785 to the Marquis de Lur Saluces (who include among their forebears the husband of the gentle Grésilidis, the one who tempted the devil). Speaking of the devil, I will show you the Satan by Leonardo da Pistoja; it's a female Satan, Madmachelle; Diornède Carafa, the Bishop of Ariano, had the artist portray his mistress with the features of Satan ... " So his erudition generated endless connections.

Catalans are always on bad terms with whichever Madrid government is in power. The Catalan Sert, on the contrary, always got on well with the authorities, whoever they were. He drove around in cars with CD number plates, sometimes he displayed the Republican colours on his houses, and sometimes the yellow and gold; he knew how to reconcile the contrasting figures of Quiñones and Lequerica;[4] he had decorated the Vickers building; he had also covered the directors' board rooms in Essen with his paintings; the Rothschilds fed him and the Germans heated his studio—Guelphs may pass, as well as Ghibellines, but art remains. Sert was passionate about great houses ... in every sense of the word: the Sassoons, Lady Ripon, the Saxton Nobles, the SDN, the Fauchiez Magnans, the Newport villas, the Palm Beach palaces did not offer sufficient spaces for his inventive, gilt-edged genius.

---

4   Two prominent members of the exiled Spanish opposition. [Tr]

Misia Sert a 1921

MISIA

F ORGET THESE BOTTICELLIS; these da Vincis, they're appalling, what rubbish!" Misia would say to me. "Let's go and
buy corals to make Chinese trees."

Whoever mentions Sert, mentions Misia.
She has been my only woman friend. (My feelings for her,
what's more, were more those of liking than of friendship.) This
obliges me therefore to describe how I see her, what she meant
to me, and what she is. I have seen her appear at the moment
of my greatest grieving: other people's grief lures her, just as
certain fragrances lure the bee.

We only like people because of their failings—Misia gave me
ample and countless reasons for liking her. Misia only devotes
herself to what she doesn't understand; yet she understands
almost everything. Me, I remained a mystery to her; out of this
came a loyalty that was always belied, but which, after some
differences, reverted to normal. She's an unusual human being,
who only appealed to women and to a few artists. Misia is to
Paris what the goddess Kali is to the Hindu pantheon. She is

simultaneously the goddess of destruction and of creation. She kills and scatters her germs, without realising. Satie called her "mother kill-all", and Cocteau "the back-street abortionist". That's unfair. Misia certainly doesn't create, but in certain dim lights, she performs her useful and kindly act like a glow-worm in the dark.

There's no denying that, in her case, she's unaware of her influence; but this Polish woman's Oriental fondness for destroying and falling asleep after the disaster, the calm soul in the midst of the ruins, is entirely conscious.

Misia has no sense of moderation. 'French rational clarity' and the 'blue line of modest hills' mean nothing to this nomad from the steppes.

She has an acute thirst for success and a deep and sacrilegious passion for failure. For herself, whom she loathes, for the man she serves, her tactical knowledge and her promotional strategy are always on the alert.

Misia loves me. "You must realise," Lifar said to me, "that Misia has done for you what she has done for no one else." It's true. She craved my affection. This love comes from a great basic generosity mixed with a devilish delight in denigrating everything she gives. Shallow people say she's "highly intelligent". If she had been, I would not have been friendly with her. I am not sufficiently intelligent for "highly intelligent" women. "We live," Misia used to say, "on a reputation for usurped intelligence."

From the age of fifteen, ever since she posed at Valvins, with her hair in curlers and her blouse rolled up, as women from a brothel for Toulouse-Lautrec, Renoir, Vuillard and Bonnard, up to the time of Picasso, Stravinsky and Diaghilev, Misia has spent fifty years living among the greatest artists and she is completely uncultured. She has never opened a book.

"Take this book, Misia."

"What for? I wonder when you find the time to read?"

She doesn't even read her own letters. She has imposed herself on all the great artists of her time, but she has lost them, for they are creators, and she deprives them of oxygen (she only sees them again so as to make sure I don't see them); she would like them to be without soul, without talent, for her alone, just as her Chinese trees are without leaves.

"Ah! How long it is!" moaned Misia at Bayreuth one day, as she was listening to *Parsifal*.

An irritated German, sitting next to her, turned to her:

"Are you sure, Madame, that it is not you who are too short?"

Misia has a sickly heart; in friendship she squints and in love she limps. And since she is intelligent enough to tolerate it, this makes her attractive. She aspires to greatness, she loves to mingle with it, to sniff it, to control it and reduce it. The sublime in art, with the deep feelings that accompany it, does credit to her. If having good taste means saying no, Misia is taste itself.

This eternal *no*, as a natural effect of divine wrath, leads Misia to surround herself with nothing but rubbish, with ghastly little trinkets, with dubious people, who are indecisive even where their sex is concerned. All she likes is mother-of-pearl; a nostalgia for vases probably. Luxury for her is the opposite of luxury. For Misia, it's the flea market.

So what about her fondness for me? I repeat that it comes from the fact that she has never been able to destroy me, that is to say prove her love to me. "She loves you, Madmachelle," Sert used to say, "because she has never been able to trick you." She was never able to find the chink in the armour, which nevertheless exists. For a quarter-of-a-century, the worm has made its way around the fruit without ever being able to get inside it. The steppe has never prevailed over the French countryside. "Monsieur le Président," Hitler said to Laval one day, "what Poland lacks is a Massif Central."

Misia believes sincerely that she loves me—it's unrequited love; seeing me makes her unhappy, but she gets fed up if she doesn't see me. My friendships make her demented and this dementia gives an irreplaceable pungency to her life. When she turns Picasso against me, she says: "I saved you from him."

Having loved her, Vuillard came to hate her. He wanted to paint my portrait; Misia made it up with him merely in order to prevent it. She is like the St Bernard who brings you back to the shore with your head under water. Misia is full of malice, in both the modern and the archaic meaning of the word.

She does everything by calculation; but if she knows how to divide and subtract, she is incapable of adding up.

She dug out some extraordinarily amusing clothes, which she kept for months, for years, and she knew how to give them a very makeshift appearance at the last moment.

She had absolutely no shame, no sense of honesty, but she had a grandeur and an innocence about her that surpassed everything one usually observes in women. (Let no one criticise me here for my harshness—for it's because of all this that I adored her.) Gaffes terrify me; Misia loves them as one would some wonderful savoury dish. So far as love is concerned, Edwards and Sert were for her what gaffes are in the social sense: gaffes that were intended, premeditated, relished; for women without sexual drive, like her, these stimulants are necessary. What allowed her to retain her Jewish soul were the Jews themselves.

In a woman there is everything, and in Misia there was every sort of woman. She has no life of her own, she lives through others. She's a parasite of the heart. Her love is atomic, it's the splitting of the love atom. If I am bored somewhere, but especially if I'm having fun, Misia comes up to me:

"I can't go on! Come home with me. We shall have fun."

Once we're in the car:

"Thank goodness we left, I was going to explode!"

And since she is a first-rate super-flirt, she soon makes me forget the place we had just left, she livens things up, she becomes marvellous, and all her virtues begin to shine.

Misia has the most serious virtue of all: she's never boring, even though she's always bored.

To distract her—everything to do with me amused her—and to inflame her curiosity, I invented bogus love affairs, imaginary passions. She was always taken in.

We were at anchor off Trieste, the time of day one whispers secrets.

"I'm returning to Venice, dear Misia, because I am suffering abominably; I'm madly in love with a man who loathes me."

The word 'suffering' elated Misia.

"There was I convinced that you had never suffered! How could you not have come and told me that earlier?"

When I threw down my cards, when I cried "April fool", when I said to her: "Seeing you were bored, my dearest, I invented this little story," Misia was appalled.

A few days later, in Venice, I almost perished from a fever; Misia was so disappointed and angry that she didn't even ask for news of me.

And another time:

"If you swear you won't repeat it, Misia, I'm going to tell you a secret."

"Go on! Go on!"

"I … I'm going to marry the Prince of Wales! But not a word!"

"I … I'm going to stay here with you, because if I go away, I'll spill everything!"

Misia is neither good nor bad: she's one of the frailties of humanity, but she's a force of nature. Her mere presence makes you want to speak badly of people. You don't feel happy leaving her house; you regret the bad things you've said. She is generous: as long as you suffer, she's ready to give everything, to give everything so that you suffer all the more.

As soon as she has spoken ill or done something harmful to someone, Misia is overcome with fear and runs over to her victim's home as a precaution, overwhelms her with kind words, and explains that it's for her own good; in short, she makes the first move. When I see her arrive, from the morning onwards, I welcome her like this:

"The things you must have said about me yesterday!"

In my case, I sometimes bite my friends, but Misia, she devours them.

Even when Misia speaks the truth, she finds a way of being amusing. I hate asking questions; I'm full of admiration for Misia's brazen interrogative manner.

Misia's tragedy is that she that she misses her opportunities, after having made everybody else miss theirs. But she miscarries only freaks. In this way all the important men, precisely because they were important, have eluded her; she has retained only what she has destroyed, that is to say nothing. There's nothing left for Madame Verdurinska but to embroider her existence, under the marvelling eye of Monsieur Boulos.

Misia has not succeeded in corroding certain indestructible French spirits. My aunt Adrienne de Nexon, who lives near us, says of her:

"I called and had tea with 'your Polish woman'."

"My Polish woman?"

"Yes, that lady who wears satin slippers in the mornings … I don't like her. She tried very cleverly to drag every secret out of me. I replied: 'Madame, do you take me for an information service? … ' You've got some strange friends … How can you get on with these foreigners who are so badly brought up?"

Les Ballets Russes
1912

RETURN TO PARIS

A FTER THESE FEW MONTHS of exhilarating freedom (I had not taken a holiday for years), I returned to Paris and moved into the Ritz, where I stayed for six years.

I took up my dictatorial life once more: success and solitude. I was exhausted by my break. Nothing relaxes me so much as work, and nothing tires me so much as doing nothing. The more I work, the more I want to work.

I cannot take orders from anyone else, except in love; and even then … Nothing had changed in my absence. In other establishments, they allow for fifty chefs and sous-chefs. With me, there is only 'Mademoiselle'. When I go away, I leave only mourners behind me. I very much respect other people's liberty, while at the same time expecting reciprocity. Liberty, alas, is a gift that terrifies people; I don't just mean theirs, but one's own.

I was working towards a new society. Up until then they had been clothes designed for women who were useless and idle, women whose lady's maids had to pass them their stockings; I now had customers who were busy women; a busy woman needs to feel comfortable in her clothes. You need to be able to roll up your sleeves. Beauty is not prettiness: why do so many mothers teach their daughters to be affected, instead of teaching them about beauty? It's true, beauty is not learnt in a flash; but by the time you have learnt through experience, beauty has faded away! It's one of the facets of the female tragedy. There are so many others, about which novelists and those 'who look into a woman's heart' are dreadfully unaware.

(May I be forgiven—it takes a great deal of courage not to see women as goddesses; and to say so!)

A man, for example, generally improves as he grows older, whereas his partner deteriorates. The face of a mature man is more beautiful than that of an adolescent. Ageing is Adam's charm and Eve's tragedy.

A woman ages badly. Look at this one, with her legs in the air, doing her physical education exercises under the glaring light of a beach umbrella.

"She's downright ugly," we would say.

And they reply to us:

"That's my grandmother."

A woman who is getting older takes more and more care of herself with every passing day; and one of the diabolical effects of inherent justice is that taking care of oneself is what ages one most. I feel sorry for those women who take rest cures with specialists who make them sit still for hours, in the darkness, in comfortable armchairs. The worst lines, those of egoism, are etched in their skin, there's nothing to be done. However much one says, so as to flatter them: "She's an angel," angels also grow old. (We'll talk about 'angels' again in a moment.) No point in patting your double chin, it's better to massage your morale.

Women today certainly look twenty years younger, they certainly continue to display unshakeable energy and behave as if they are never going to die, but nature always prevails over their efforts.

"How lovely Pauline looked, yesterday evening!" people continue to say, out of habit. And nobody dares say, or even think:

"No; she's old and ugly."

Beauty endures, prettiness passes. Yet no woman wants to be beautiful; they all want to be ever so pretty.

Bemoaning one's fate is to cradle complacently the child that continues to live within every one of us, and who is of no interest to anyone. As for the real secret, which is to transform physical beauty into moral beauty, it's the one trick which most women are incapable of performing.

If they were even distressed about this, that would be their salvation. But they are so sure of themselves!

A distressed woman doesn't exist.

"I'm a little bit too plump … "

"I'm not all that plump … "

And the young encourage her in her false security. It's the swan song. Young people's compliments are delightful, as long as one resists them. Accepting them, that's a serious matter.

In any case, it's not so much a question of being young or old, as being on the right or the wrong side. I can call that a good or a bad painting: it's original, functional, indelible. There are no human beings who are not original and interesting, as long as one has taken care not to teach them anything. There is good painting everywhere, in the trains, in the convoys of emigrants, but you have to know how to see it, to read it. Where women lose out is in having been taught; where the prettiest lose out is in having been taught not just that they are pretty, but in being taught how to be pretty.

People talk about physical care: but where is the moral care? Beauty treatments should begin with the heart and the soul, otherwise cosmetics are pointless.

Moral behaviour, the art of presenting oneself with charm, taste, intuition, people's inner sense of life, none of these things can be taught. From a very young age, we are fully formed; education can change nothing. It is useless having teachers, teachers have lost many more men (and women, especially) than they have produced. Clemenceau's remark about Poincaré: "He knows everything and understands nothing", coupled with his remark about Briand: "He knows nothing and understands everything", remains true, and always will.

Another axiom: there are intelligent women, but there are no intelligent women at a couturier's. (Nor moral women; they would sell their soul for a dress.)

Mirrors no longer exist for the woman who is growing older. She replaces the mirror with conceit. It is true that when one reaches fifty, everything becomes difficult. A highly intelligent woman with a head of grey hair tells me:

"I'm calling it a day. Make me an outfit that I can wear from now until I die."

"It's impossible," I reply to her. "A woman who is growing older must be in fashion; only a young woman can be in *her* fashion."

Women should age with the times we live in, not with their own. People say to them: "Take this," (which means: "In this black dress, people will see you have been beautiful"). But they don't listen … The tragedy of the ageing woman is that she suddenly remembers that light blue suited her when she was twenty.

"Make me an old lady's dress," Hélène Morand says to me.

"There are no more old ladies," I reply.

The shops see women as they ought to be; dressmakers' salons see women as they are.

"Dora, Daisy, Dorothea, Diane, she's an angel!" say their friends.

The angel returns her dress, having worn it at a soirée where everyone could admire it; the angel returns it saying that she had ordered a red velvet gown when in fact she had ordered it in black, as can be proved by the purchase order, signed by her.

The angel accompanies a friend to the fitting:

"This white velvet dress is pretty, but it's not your style … "

"I had it made for the Rothschilds' ball."

"Trust me, come to Lelong's instead. You'll be another woman." (How charming!)

The friend begs us to take the dress back. The next day the angel appears who had been unable to sleep thinking of her friend's dress.

"That white velvet dress which was returned to you yesterday, I'll take it, but you'll have to sell it to me at half-price. It's a sale item. OK?"

The angel always says: "OK?"

Sometimes the angel, having created a great deal of publicity about the clothes she had made for her, reappears at the fashion show and whispers in customers' ears:

"Don't make any decision, my dear, without having seen the Molyneux collection."

If I am only too familiar with this last glint of romanticism, the Angel, so dear to Gide and to Giraudoux, it is because I have heard what the sales assistants say. Our sales assistants, generally former models, know their jobs, which they adore, wonderfully well. They know how to listen, to listen on their feet; they know the right time to sit down. They are the best confidantes (a woman is always frightened that her lady's maid may blackmail her; but she has total trust in her sales assistant). The sales assistant has the enormous privilege of hearing the angel's confessions.

"Should I leave him?"

"Does he love me?"

"What would Vera think of him? Is it a good match?" (and other equally banal and heavenly remarks …)

While they are recounting their life stories to the sales assistants (the women are all gossips), the sales assistant is not selling and the fitter is getting impatient; three dressmakers are waiting on the fifth floor. But the angel thinks only of herself. The angel does not know the price of time. The angel has a dress that suits her perfectly well, but wants to be able to say, at a smart lunch party:

"I must go round to Chanel's."

She returns again once, twice, three times, to no avail. Out of pure sadism the angel manages to prevent the sales assistant from continuing her job on another floor, which is to sell dresses and earn her commission, and to keep her unoccupied for an entire day.

At this point I must stop these stories from the fitting room.

I believe I have raised dressmaking to a certain level of importance. The purpose of my relating this is to say so and not to spread gossip.

I conclude by observing that one has to have experienced the company of women in order to know what a woman is like. The angel is a creature without any scruples, a real man-eater.

The angel is not bothered about pleasing; she thinks only of money. To the angel who believes I am a businesswoman and who asks me for financial tips, I reply:

"I am not Madame Hanau. Marthe Letellier, the greatest beauty of the pre-1914 period, thought of nothing but the Stock Exchange. The Marquise de J doesn't need a footstool at Court, she wants an armchair in front of the *tap* at Saint-Phalle's. And yet she's an angel, and everyone in her circle is agreed on this. An angel never pays in cash, however (in my business, paying cash is like paying in instalments). An angel pays on the never-never."

The angel, who is now a widow (for angels have a sex) and who, dressed in mourning, gives a grand dinner party:

"He would have hated me to be bored … "

Or:

"Come to dinner; we'll talk about him … "

The theosophical angel:

"My religion forbids me to mourn."

Man has a certain ingenuousness, but woman has none; as for the angel, it's capable of everything. The angel knows it cannot be killed because it is immortal; it knows it cannot be put in prison, because it has wings.

Society (with very rare exceptions, under Marie-Antionette or under the Empress Eugénie) took notice of invitations from the fashion houses, but none of the couturiers themselves. After the last war—I mention this because all Parisians know it—I was much sought after. Sought after, but not easily found, for I continued scarcely ever to go out in the evening; I could count on my fingers the number of grand dinner parties or receptions I attended. Ten years later, you could see many of my colleagues mixing in social circles. In another ten years there will be scarcely any couturiers' salons: there will just be society couturiers, and we will hurry along to the Dior ball, to the Patou cocktail party.

Since I went out very little, I needed to be kept informed about what was going on in the houses where my dresses were displayed; so I began the practice, which was then unprecedented, of surrounding myself with people of quality to act as a liaison between myself and society, between the inside and the outer world. Englishwomen from high society, from the Russian, Italian and French aristocracy, came to work at rue Cambon. People said I was an anarchist and that I took an evil pleasure in humiliating people of standing, by placing them under my command. A great many foolish remarks have been made on this subject.

The Ballets Russes had jolted the world of dance; October 1917 had jolted the whole of Russia, and Paris became filled with émigrés. Bravely, they started to look for work, just as our own people did, in London and St Petersburg, after 1793. I employed some of them; I have always felt immensely sorry for princes of royal blood; their job, when they are able to carry it out, is the saddest there is, and when they are unable to carry it out, that's worse. Furthermore, Russians fascinated me. Inside everyone from the Auvergne there is an Oriental one doesn't realise is there—the Russians revealed the Orient to me.

It has been said that "every woman should have a Romanian in her life". I would add: every Westerner should have succumbed to 'Slavic charm' to know what it is. I was captivated. Their notion of "everything that is yours is mine" thrilled me. All Slavs are naturally refined, and the most humble ones are never common.

Feodorowna came to work at rue Cambon. One day, I discovered her in tears. She explained, in between sobs, that she owed a lot of money and that, in order to pay off her debt, she had to give herself to a monster, a horrible frizzy-haired, flabby-lipped oil tycoon; of the two dishonours she would choose the latter.

"How much do you need?"

"Thirty-thousand francs."

"Thirty-thousand francs to sleep with someone is expensive," I said; "but for not sleeping with him, it's dirt cheap. Here you are, I'll lend it to you." (I used the word 'lend' without any delusions; one does not lend to Russians. But giving brings bad luck; if small gifts maintain a friendship, expensive gifts compromise it.)

A few days later, Feodorowna invited me to her home. It was dusk, there were mauve lampshades on the parquet floor, a balalaika, caviar in a block of ice, vodka in carafes, Gypsies: in short, one of those island nights that Russians love to recreate everywhere. I was enchanted. The idea that my friend had escaped from the clutches of the Caucasian monster delighted me.

But with all this nocturnal glamour, I wondered whether my loan had covered the costs.

"Did you make use of the thirty-thousand francs?"

"What could I do ... I felt so sad ... I wanted to have a bit of fun first ... I kept it ... I bought this caviar with ... "

I never saw the money again, but it was not long before I saw Feodorowna again in the company of the oil tycoon, whom she adored and whom she soon left for a far more monstrous Czech.

Sergei Diaghilev

DIAGHILEV

MISIA NEVER LEFT Diaghilev's side; between them it was one of those whispered, doting relationships, spiteful, affectionate, riddled with snares, in which Serge found his pleasures, his social contacts, his conveniences, his necessities, and in which Misia found the one remedy for her boredom. With Diaghilev she didn't pout any more (Misia's famous pout).

From the day I first met him, until the day I closed his eyelids, I have never seen Serge take a rest.

"I could have earned millions if I had put on *Petrushka* again, and lived off *Schéhérazade* as others did from *Le Miracle* or *Die Fledermaus*, but I prefer my pleasures."

As he spoke he kept reassuring himself, with his heavily ringed hand, that his large black pearl was properly in place on his pearl-grey cravat. After the Ballets, he came to my home to have a quick supper, without removing that pelisse made from the pelts of Siberian animals and strapped with frogging in which Cocteau caricatured him so often; without taking off his white gloves, he took a chocolate. Then he succumbed, finished the box, his fat cheeks and his heavy chin wobbling as he munched, made himself ill, and stayed chatting all night.

An extraordinary prospector of the wells of European genius, a purveyor on a Balzac-like scale of dance, music and painting, which until then were unknown, a white-flecked intriguer offering the Orient to the West. In Spain he discovered Falla, and in St Petersburg a young student of Rimsky's by the name of Stravinsky; in Arcueil, Satie.

He was the most delightful of friends. I loved his zest for life, his passions, his scruffiness, so different from the sumptuous figure of legend, the days spent without eating, the nights spent rehearsing, living in a theatre seat, destroying himself by putting his all into the show. He introduced the best painters to the best musicians, he taught the French public, those who out of snobbery were willing to make Arabian Nights journeys, that there were unknown enchanters at the corner of the street, Dukas, Schmitt, Ravel, Picasso, Derain. He shook Montparnasse out of its jabbering and opened up the debate to the public at large, made them interested in it and transformed it. Stubborn, generous, mean, then a spendthrift all of a sudden, never knowing beforehand what he was going to do, buying priceless paintings for nothing, giving them away, allowing them to be stolen from him, he travelled through Europe in the role of penniless patron, his trousers held up by a couple of safety pins. One evening, in Venice, between the two columns, he spoke to us about his childhood, about his friend Benois, about the St Petersburg School of Art, about his father, General Diaghilev, about his arrival in Paris, in that heroic period when he was exhibiting icons, or giving concerts of Russian historical music.

"Moussorgsky … " Misia would say (the pout reappears).

"Of course, not Prokofiev! You have to begin gently."

I can see him with that air of a furry cat that enjoys its food, his thick lips opened wide in laughter, his drooping jowls, the glint of mockery in his eye beneath his monocle, with its black braid blowing in the wind.

Russia was moving forwards stealthily. 1910, classical and sophisticated. *Le Spectre, Les Sylphides*. And then Nijinsky comes and batters down our doors, like those of a harem. Pink and mauve posters suggestive of his leaps, signed by Cocteau, cover the walls of Paris. The earth trembles beneath the rhythm of the archers from *Igor*. One wondered what was being put in motion … Young lords lounged languidly in the aisles of the Châtelet, as did certain of our new Stendhals—Giradoux, who wore a monocle at the time, jealously guarding Monsieur de Balzac's walking-stick, Emile Henriot and Vaudoyer, twin brothers disguised as knights of Orsay, Mauriac, his hands clasped together, wearing the blue uniform of the ambulance service created by Etienne de Beaumont, a young man from Bordeaux who was unable to sleep on account of the Parisian Cocteau's successes, and for whom no honour would alleviate his provincial complexes—all were in raptures about the essential colours and about the harmonies of tones. As for Diaghilev, he got straight down to business. His business was to make Russia known subconsciously, to assert his Russian faith; with his handsome slaves, who hung on his success, following in his wake, he behaved like a Turkish despot.

Diaghilev was an extraordinary acrobat, a recreator of talent and an entertainer of genius. Had he brought to France companies such as the Imperial Theatre Ballet, he would merely have earned a *succès d'estime*. (The more so since he had only restored to Paris what St Petersburg had once borrowed from her.) But he did better; he invented a Russia for abroad, and, naturally, abroad was taken in. (*Petrushka* and *Schéhérazade* were not shown in St Petersburg until ten years after they were seen in Paris.) Since everything in the theatre was only trompe l'oeil, false perspectives were necessary: the Russia of the Ballets Russes succeeded in the theatre precisely because it was built on fictional material.

In 1918, when he had exhausted this seam, Diaghilev changed his style completely, with the introduction of comedy into dance (Massine and *Les Femmes de bonne humeur*, *Pulcinella* with Picasso, after *Parade*). For five years, served well by *les Six*, he rediscovered his youth; and posterity may be more grateful to him for having created *Les Biches*, *Les Fâcheux* and *Matelots* than for *Les Sylphides* or *Le Spectre*, for having inspired Etienne de Beaumont's *Soirées à Paris* and given birth to the Swedes.

The flighty, frivolous, fickle Diaghilev was the first to understand that you had to grab hold of masterpieces, that nothing prevented you from dancing in circles so much as dance music did (it's true that Isadora Duncan dancing to a Beethoven symphony had been a precursor), that you could dance to a painting by Picasso, to Dada ideas, to Claudel's poetry. Börlin wanted to go even further in this direction, and he came a cropper, but Diaghilev, who was taste itself, never put a step wrong, precisely because he was light-footed. He nearly devised a ballet out of the 1913 riots based on *Sacré*, that *Hernani* of our times! After Serge, they danced among black statues, in the ruins of factories of futurism, in museums, to Velasquez and to Berlioz, to Bach and to Handel, to Shakespeare and to Paul Valéry. I know all the criticisms people have made about him, that he tackles dance from the outside, that he subordinates it to other art forms, etc, but one fact remains: Diaghilev dominated his age, and his age, which has been that of Nijinsky, Massine, Lifar, la Pavlova, the Sakharoffs, Argentina, the rebirth of the music hall, negro dance steps, rhythmics and explosive rhythm, etc, was probably the most brilliant period that dance has ever known.

I can see him as he was when he was alive, and how lively he was. He rides roughshod over scores. He hacks into them, without knowing whether it's dance music. He picks out the best bits, as a gourmet might. He succeeds in the impossible. He ruins himself after having gone *banco*. He tears at his lock of white hair. He rushes over to Princesse Edmond's house; he rushes over to Maud Cunard's; he explains that he needs a thousand pounds, that very evening, that the creditors have seized control, that the curtain won't rise; he wrings his hands; diabetes makes his forehead perspire.

"I went to see the Princess. She gave me seventy-five thousand francs!"

"She's a grand American lady," I say. "I'm only a French dress designer, but here is two hundred thousand."

With the money in his pocket, he plunges back into the adventure the next day, he disappears, beset by romantic dramas that are as relentless as they are tortuous, and he emerges from the shadows or from America with a new musician and with his eightieth ballet.

Diaghilev sometimes told me about his experiences in Switzerland, during the First World War. He was rehearsing in Lausanne, in a hangar; Stravinsky was working with Ramuz next door; Lenin and Trotsky were waiting on the shores of Lake Leman for the moment when they were to return to Russia, through Germany, in a sealed carriage. 1917. *Parade* and revolution. The Châtelet and the Poutiloff factories. When I bring together these similar Russias that were unaware of each other, I think that they amount to one and the same thing.

The years go by. He continues to put his trust in genius, to search for genius, as a tramp searches for cigarette butts on a pavement.

In Venice, on his way back from Salzburg, in front of our very eyes, Diaghilev has just died. Present are Catherine d'Erlanger, Misia, Boris Kochno, Lifar.

"My friends, my only friends … it seems to me that I am drunk … "

The next day, a long procession of gondolas leaves the Orthodox *dei Grecchi* church and makes its way towards the San Michele cemetery, where the cypresses rise above the pink walls bordered in white.

"What will become of the Ballets?"

"Who can take them on again?"

"Nobody."

I did not prevent Diaghilev's ballets from collapsing, as people have said. I had never seen *Le Sacre du printemps* before 1914. Serge spoke about it as if it had caused a scandal and had been a great historical moment. I wanted to hear it and to offer to subsidise it. I don't regret the three hundred thousand francs that it cost me.

Serge stirred up a world full of ideas, colours, passions and of banknotes: all he left was a pair of cuff links which Lifar would swap for his own at the moment he was placed in the coffin.

MADAME DE CHÉVIGNÉ

I HAD A DELIGHTFUL OLD FRIEND, the Comtesse Adhéaume de Chévigné. When I lived in the Faubourg Saint-Honoré, she was staying in the rue d'Anjou, almost opposite me. In this rue d'Anjou salon, in about 1900, all the most respected 'clubmen' and elegant women in Paris, from the other faubourg, had streamed by, in the days when one took lunch at half-past eleven, when one called on people at three o'clock, before social gatherings took place, and where the gentlemen came in and sat down, with their top hats on their knees. With her red wig, her loud, hoarse voice that delighted Marcel Proust, her authoritarian manners and her peremptory tone of voice, Madame de Chévigné was a character out of Saint-Simon, parodied by Swann. She looked like an elderly actress; or more accurately, it was Madame de Chévigné whom Marguerite Deval, Moreno, Pauline Carton and all those actresses who specialised in playing the parts of ridiculous old women, down through her son-in-law, Francis de Croisset, did their best to copy. What with the actresses imitating the countess, and she, imitating them in turn, they were soon inextricable.

Madame de Chévigné was the first woman in the world to have said *merde*.

Her conversation was intoxicating; it was a chronicle, a memoir, an end-of-year revue …

"Today, my dear, young women are ignorant and foolish. Men don't teach them anything any more. Not even the social graces. In our case, we knew men who had no need to learn manners, they were born into them … I learnt everything I know through making love. A lover teaches you those sorts of things, not a husband. My lover used to take me to the Louvre. You can't spend your whole time … kissing one another! You've got to like those things … As for being hot-blooded, well, Cécile[5] and I were certainly hot-blooded … But you have moments of leisure, even in bachelors' apartments. I'm talking of a time when people had bachelors' apartments and you wore a veil to go in; nowadays, people do it anywhere, on top of anything, between two doors, in front of the servants. Look, take my daughter (that one, my youngest one, now I can swear that she is certainly by Monsieur de Chévigné. What's more all my children are Adhéaume's. No bastards, whatever happens!). Well, my daughter has been learning since she was three years old, now she's sixty and she doesn't know a thing!

"You don't have to learn in order to know, Madame; Misia, for instance, is considered to be a great musician yet I've never heard her play more than four chords by Chopin.

"Let's talk about her! She adores the Jews. Furthermore, my dear, Misia lives in the ghetto; look at all those members of the chosen race she has dragged around behind her, Thadée Natanson, Bernstein, Edwards, Alfred Savoir … Me, I've got nothing against Jews … And I've got plenty to prove it. To put it plainly, at the time of Félix Faure, the Rothschilds, they didn't count for much … at

---

5   Princesse J Murat

the Jockey, my dear, there was only Haas,[6] and even then, he had been elected in '71, during the Commune, one afternoon when there was no one there to blackball him … "

Madame de Chévigné died shortly before the war. For some years she had not been receiving visitors. Her door was only open to her family, to close friends, to me. If Misia came to see her, she would only have her brought in so that she could speak to her harshly, to her face.

"You wouldn't understand that, you who know everything!"

And she would wink surreptitiously at me, click her tongue, and give me a mischievous kick under the table, without Misia realising.

"In 18—, we knew how to behave. F— loved me; or so I thought. One day, after a journey, I arrive on the arm of Monsieur de Chévigné for a grand dinner party. In the anteroom, I cast my eyes over the list of guests. I read: Comte and Comtesse de F. The fickle fellow had got married without telling me. I feel flustered … but all of a sudden I pull myself together, and I say to myself: 'You are Laure de Chévigné, née Sade.' (Sade! What a lovely name … Misia would sigh. What would I not give to be born Sade!)

"We're French, we are! These foreigners, they think they know it all! Can't stand the Russians … I was in Petersburg … I stayed with the Grand-Duchess Vladimir. People are polite over there, too polite. You're treated well in Russia, but they don't respect you; they give you presents with diamonds, but they use you as they would an object. And then, their wealth, I went to Tsarskoe Selo, and it wasn't as smart as all that!"

---

6   Swann

Occasionally Auguste, the elderly servant, would come in.

"What is it now, Auguste?"

"Madame la Comtesse, it's Madame X."

"Could you not have said that I was unwell? I am with Mademoiselle."

"Madame la Comtesse, I can't lie."

"Then why are you a servant? Servants are supposed to say no."

Worried that I might weary the Comtesse, Auguste returned a little while later.

"Madame la Comtesse should think about dinner."

"Leave me alone! I'm having fun! That fellow wants to force-feed me! He gives me my soup; he thinks he can do as he pleases! I'm not doddery, but he's convinced I am! What were we saying? That Misia didn't know three notes of Chopin? Reynaldo, by Jove, now there's a musician! In Venice, my dear, Madame de Vantalis would arrange for a piano to be put on the gondola for him; the moon, the Grand Canal, and off we go, with everyone following. And Madrazo! Coco, have you heard Madrazo singing '*la Tour Saint-Jacques*'? It was quite different from Jacques Février! … What was I telling you … Remind me please, I no longer know where I am, because of that idiot, Auguste … Ah yes, we were talking about the young women of today … They're all tarts! And worse! (In my day, even the tarts had manners.) Have you noticed that nowadays women don't even know how to walk into a drawing room? Shall I show you how they introduce themselves?"

There followed an imitation by the Comtesse, who had leapt out of bed, of a woman of today, slightly awkward and slightly pretentious, who is always clumsy and 'coarse'.

"In our day, we cut a better figure! Do you call that making an entrance? Well, look!"

After this violent exercise, Madame de Chévigné went back to bed, out of breath.

"I'm short of breath, my dear. My heart's packing in … "

I reassured her that it was simply lack of fitness. She turned her gaunt, tragic old clown's mask towards me, with its Punchinello nose, its downturned mouth, and her muted, gruff voice that seemed to come from beneath the ground:

"My children have forced me to leave rue d'Anjou; I lived there for forty years; I have obeyed; but I know very well it will bring me bad luck: one only leaves one's home to die. I'll die because of it. If I feel better, if I can go out, ask me round. But not with old people, whatever you do. Invite me with the young. Otherwise, come back and see me. I'll talk to you about Madame Standish (née des Cars) and about Madame Greffulhe. Those were women, they were! They knew how to curtsey. At Fordsdorf I watched them curtseying, it was quite different … "

"Auguste, drive Mademoiselle home … You're very likely to find me in bed again next time. You see, at my age, when a woman has removed her corset and her hairpiece, my dear, she never puts them on again!"

The day came, in fact, when Madame de Chévigné did grow weak. Marie-Thérèse de Croisset came to tell me:

"Maman is very ill. She thinks she's at your house … "

A few days later, I went to her burial.

Picasso dans les années 2...

PICASSO

WHEN PICASSO LIVED IN MONTROUGE, during the last war, some burglars broke into his home; they only took clothes and didn't bother about his paintings. Today clothes cost much more than they did in 1915, but Picasso's canvases have increased far more than clothing material. No burglar would make the same mistake again. '*Il y a les toiles de maîtres et les mètres de toile*', as Labiche puts it.[7]

I don't know whether he is a genius; it's hard to say whether someone you see a lot is a genius; but I am certain that he is somewhere on that invisible chain which links geniuses to one another over the centuries.

Years, decades have passed and Picasso is still alive, very much alive. The wave on which he rode has not receded. He is neither forgotten, nor has he become an idol, which is equally serious. He has retained his intelligence, his acrobat's reflexes, his Basque suppleness, for he is Basque through his father, the drawing teacher.

---

7   Eugène Labiche (1815–1888). French playwright who observed in minute detail the foibles and fashions of Second Empire society. The pun on the words *maîtres* and *mètres* is untranslatable. [Tr]

I have maintained a strong friendship with him. I think it is reciprocated. We have not changed, in spite of upheavals. Twenty years ago, everything was delightful, for many reasons, but mainly because not everything was in the public domain, because the burglars of Montrouge did not know who Picasso was, because politics did not poison art.

I get on very well with strong personalities. With great artists, I am very respectful and very free at the same time; I am their conscience. If they disappear into the pages of *Harper's Bazaar*, I tell them. I retain my critical faculties. If I find myself choking with admiration, then it means they are not truly great artists.

"I protected you from Picasso," Misia said.

I had no need of being protected from anyone except from Misia. For where Misia has once loved, the grass doesn't grow any more. Picasso set himself the huge task of making a clean sweep of everything, but I wasn't on the path of his vacuum cleaner. I liked the man. In reality it was his painting that I liked, even though I didn't understand anything about it. I was convinced and I enjoy being so. Picasso, for me, is like a logarithms table.

He destroyed, but then he constructed. He arrived in Paris in 1900, when I was a child, already able to draw like Ingres, whatever Sert said. I am almost old and Picasso is still working; he has become the radioactive principle of painting. Our meeting could only have happened in Paris (people don't live in the Auvergne, and you don't spend your life in Malaga, or in Barcelona).

When I knew him, he had returned from Rome with Satie and Cocteau. It was *Parade*; his famous cardboard cut-out 'managers' were shuffling rhythmically across the stage of the Châtelet. He was emerging from cubism and gummed papers. I was later involved with the revolutions that periodically shook the rue de La Boétie. I witnessed the success of his designs and the public acclaim, one after the other, of *Le Tricorne* and *Pulcinella*.

I would often climb up to his alchemist's den. I saw Apollinaire make his appearance and pass him by, the gatherings in rue Huyghens and rue Ravignan, both at first hand or from what Reverdy or Max Jacob told me. I saw him stop being the exclusive property of Manolo and Paysan, of Grenwitz and Baron Mollet, to become the equal of Stalin and Roosevelt. I saw Ambroise Vollard and Rosenberg hovering around the treasure-house that produced treasures. I saw Cocteau on his path of seduction, Dada flirting, the surrealists showering praise on him. I saw the Modiglianis and the Juan Gris come and go, and Picasso remain. Apollinaire said of him that his inner rhythm had the monotony of Arab rhythm. The centuries pass, the civilisations crumble, Allah remains great and Picasso is his prophet. He is also a demon. He will come back to disturb generations of young painters at the séance tables. When he goes to the Louvre, his guitars will frighten people, and at night, the duty watchman and his statues will set off in the darkness, despite the patrols, to walk around the Egyptian gallery.

Coco dans les
années 20

FORAIN

ORAIN AND I GOT ON WELL. I was young and defenceless. There was a suspension of hostilities. He took charge of my education. He took me to the cabaret. With his crooked mouth, his beady eye, his acute sensitivity, open-hearted as always, using his vocal cords as he would the string of a bow, and pierced himself by as many arrows as he fired, Forain made me understand that Paris of a quarter-of-a-century ago, which, in its resonances and small proportions, still resembled the Paris of the Second Empire.

"Do you like Mother Edwards? Don't trust those sorts of people. They're bastards! It doesn't suit you … My girl, the human species is not very nice … I'm told you go around with queers … I'm telling you one last time: fairies, they're all bastards!"

He would go on like that all day long. It was July. He couldn't stop walking the streets. I was delayed because of my dress collection. Paris in July is delightful. Everything is lovely and empty, the Parisians who are there for the day have left. One has the city to oneself.

"Let's go and have dinner. I won't leave you again … What is it now? Is that you, Jean-Loup?" (Forain's son emerged.) "What do you want?"

"Papa, give me some cash."

"No."

Forain put on his overcoat and wound his Bruant-style scarf around his neck.

"Papa, give me some cash … "

"Sh—!"

Forain polished his spectacles and put them to soak in turpentine.

"Papa, give me some cash … "

The father's face suddenly lit up:

"Isn't he nice?"

"Yes," I said to please him, "your son is charming."

Forain's love for Jean-Loup sparkled, like a fire you blow on.

"Really? You find him charming?"

We went to dinner. I talked to him about Marie Laurencin, in whose work the Groults then held exclusive rights.

"Her painting, it's like some dreary needlework … She stitches soles together … "

He relaxed, his mouth grew less bitter, and he asked me to sing him a song. He especially liked this one:

Il monta sur la montagne
Pour entendre le canon
Le canon tonna si fort
Qu'il fit dans son pantalon … [8]

---

8   He climbed up the mountain/ To listen to the gun / The gun roared so loudly/ That he soiled his trousers. [Tr]

It was at Gaufres. He grabbed Georges Hugo at the bar, by the tail of his English sportscoat, made of thick, checked material, like a horse blanket!

"Listen to this, Georges:

Le canon tonna si fort …

He taught me about life:

"Never trust stupid people; choose people who are dishonest instead."

Or again:

"Be careful of drug addicts. Drugs don't make people nasty, but they bring out the nastiness."

We parted:

"I want to paint your portrait. Come to the studio."

I went to Forain's home. I was about to climb up to the second floor. But, at the first floor, I was grabbed by Madame Forain.

"I really must paint your portrait … " she said to me.

She wouldn't let me go. Forain was waiting for me impatiently, on the landing.

"You were stopped on the way by Madame Forain, eh, admit it. Did she want to prevent you from sitting for me? She'll pay for that, the bitch!"

Forain was blowing his nose on a red handkerchief.

"I'm going to tell you the latest thing she did, I'm going to tell you what she found … She went through my pockets … she got hold of my love letters … She didn't breathe a word to me about them, but she simply glued them to her fan! At a certain point, during a grand dinner party, she opened her fan, in front of everybody … "

Cécile
Sorel

FAUBOURG SAINT-HONORÉ

I T WAS AT ABOUT THIS TIME that I left the Ritz Hotel and moved into the Faubourg Saint-Honoré.

People said of the way the place was furnished that it was in England that I learnt about luxurious decor. That's wrong; luxury, for me, meant the house of my uncle from Issoire, and that has remained with me: fine Auvergne furniture 'polished by age', dark, heavy woods from the countryside, purple cherry wood, pear wood that was black beneath its sheen, rather like Spanish credence tables or Flemish sideboards, Boulle clocks in a tortoiseshell stand, cupboards with shelves that bent under the weight of clothes. I had thought that my childhood was a modest one, but I realise it was sumptuous. In Auvergne, everything was real, everything was big.

So you see, when I arrived in Paris, I wasn't particularly over-awed. It was people who amazed me, not their furnishings. I wanted to meet Cécile Sorel, about whom the contributors to *l'Illustration* (Christmas issue) engrossed their country readers. Capel took me to her house. It was some time in 1916. Sitting at the table was a woman who did not take her eyes off me: it was Misia. I was seated next to Sert. I liked Sorel, but the unpolished woodwork seemed to me to be made of plaster, the gold tablecloth was not gold, and was dirty what's more; they had casually placed fruit over the stains to make it look like a garden of Eden. The silverware was even less polished than the furniture.

Opposite me, the lady with the little chignon in the shape of a shell, with a sort of mandarin orange stuck on the top of her head, seized hold of me after dinner, and never left me.

"I also overlook the river, a few doors along. Come and see me."

Misia lived above the *Journal officiel* (she really did) on the second and top floor of a small, ancient house on the corner of the rue de Beaune. When I saw all that pile of objects, I thought she must be an antique-dealer. Capel, who came with me, thought so too. He asked, quite shamelessly: "Is it for sale?" Those fish in aquariums, those ships in bottles, those negroes made of spun glass, those windows full of fans with steel sequins, overlooking the Place Royale; I was appalled. It smelt of filth downstairs; there was no surface upon which you could use a duster or apply any polish; scarcely a flurry from that horrible object, the feather duster, which fortunately one only sees nowadays beneath the arm of servants in the first acts of plays. There was the same doctrine of clutter at Catherine d'Erlanger's home; it wends its way along walls, piles up underneath tables, proliferates on the stairs, the cupboards no longer shut ... Where was I? There: I've caught my train of thought again. When, later on, I lived in England, I rediscovered the luxury of my uncle from Issoire, oak furniture polished with white wax, large pieces of furniture, real ones, the tranquillity of the Middle Ages. The interior of a home is the natural projection of the soul, and Balzac was right to attach as much importance to it as he did to clothing.

And so I furnished the Faubourg Saint-Honoré. Plush carpet everywhere, '*colorado claro*' in colour, with silky tints, like good cigars, woven to my specifications, and brown velvet curtains with gold braiding that looked like coronets girdled in yellow silk from Winston's. I never discussed prices; only my friends protested, and Misia pulled out her hair in despair. Polovtzoff had bought a Savonnerie carpet from the Duc de C, for one hundred thousand francs.

Coco joue

1922

I 'VE KNOWN MANY CELEBRITIES, those on the wane and those up and coming. If I speak of them, it is not so as to hitch my wagon to their train, but because I have preferred their company to all others. And because those who have come to know me, even when we have been acquaintances for twenty years, make me laugh.

After my days spent working in the rue Cambon, interrupted by a hurried tea at Fleurs, in the Faubourg Saint-Honoré, I didn't much feel like going out. Yet Paris, at that time, was experiencing its strangest and most brilliant years. London and New York (I'm not talking about Berlin, which was buckling then under the throes of devaluation, hunger and expressionism) had their eyes trained on us. From the rue Cambon to Montparnasse, I watched as the Faubourg Saint-Germain attuned itself, princesses opened tea shops that bore the names of well-known books, the White Russians landed, and Europe patched things up for one last time as best it could. The Philippe Berthelots threw their final glittering party—after his reconciliation with the Tiger,[9] at the end of the Peace Conference, Philippe, in spite of Poincaré, was very much back in good favour; this had ceased under Millerand, but it was

---

9   Georges Clemenceau's nickname [Tr]

still the case, nonetheless; supported by Bailby, by his brother André, by Bader, Léon Blum, Misia, and by his old friends, he still continued to be something of the force he had been under Briand, during the first two years of the war.

I still remember a delightful Christmas Eve party at rue Cambon. Cocteau had brought along '*les Six*'. The young group of student musicians, led by Satie, was at the height of the fame it enjoyed in the early days of Le Boeuf sur le toit. Poulenc had just discarded his soldier's uniform, Auric was in love with Irène Lagut, Honegger and Darius Milhaud, who was not yet a family man, already had, as they say, a good 'grounding' behind them, even though Milhaud was not yet the Saint-Saëns of that generation. There were thirty or so of us: Germaine Taillefer, looking cool and beautiful, Jane Bathori, Ricardo Vinès, Stravinsky, Morand, Segonzac, Sert, Misia, Godebski and the Philippe Berthelots. Fargue arrived, ushering in Ravel; Philippe, his high, curly-haired forehead motionless, was threatening to recite *La Légende des siècles*, Cocteau had brought along his jazz music from Gaya's, Segonzac was doing imitations of peasants, and Hélène Berthelot, in a Chinese silk dress, looked as if she was at the foyer of the Oeuvre theatre. Satie was talking to me about a ballet. He suddenly stopped speaking, for Misia, with her brioche on her head, looking anxious and sniffing some dark intrigue, was approaching his chair. Satie, his hand covering his twisted mouth and his goatee beard, his pince-nez dangling, whispered to me:

"Here comes the cat, let's hide our birds ... "

Cocteau was describing how he had been at the Lycée Condorcet with Mistinguett's son, "nowadays a doctor with a large beard, who lives in Brazil".

vous vouliez me méchante Coco

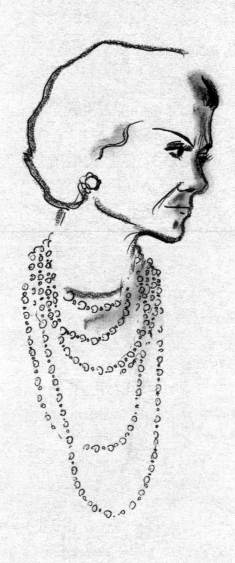

Coco peu avant la guerre

THE SIMPLE LIFE

THE MOST COMPLICATED MAN I EVER knew was Paul Iribe. He criticised me for not being simple. (By that remark alone, ever since Jean-Jacques' day, you can recognise a complex human being.) I thought I was. Deep down, perhaps I'm not? Simplicity does not mean walking around barefoot or wearing clogs, it comes from the spirit, it springs from the heart.

"I don't understand," he said, "why you need so many rooms ... What's the point of all these objects? Your way of life is ruining you. What a waste! Why do you need all these servants? One eats too well in your house. I'd come here more often, I might live close to you, if you knew how to be happy with nothing. I loathe pointless gestures, vast expenditure and complicated human beings."

Filled with the hypocritical desire to refine my needs and a sincere wish to be pleasant to him, I replied:

"So be it. I shall become simple. I shall reduce my standard of living."

Not far from the rue Cambon, I found a 'family house' in which I rented two rooms. Since this modest accommodation did not include any bathrooms, I had one built. I installed another, arranged my favourite books, a coromandel screen, two heaters and a few fine rugs. When he saw me leaving my house, Iribe was annoyed, jealous, unhappy.

"I'm boarding out," I told him. "It's very convenient; I'm round the corner from my home and I'm going to start living the famous simple life."

"Does it amuse you," he said, "to play the *midinette?*"

I told him that he was responsible for all these changes. I was waiting for him, too, to rent some modest room, since he loved the simple life so much. But he did nothing of the kind and asked me irritably:

"Are you happy?"

"Very happy."

"What are you playing at? Do you plan to stay there for long?"

I put on an act.

"You wanted me to leave the wood panelling, the marble and the wrought iron—here's my cottage. The concierge does her cooking on the stairs. Your feet knock into empty milk bottles. Isn't this the life you wanted me to lead and that you youself want to lead?"

"Do you think I'm used to living in such hovels?" he said in disgust.

And he moved in to the Ritz, opposite me.

My relationship with Iribe was a passionate one. How I loathe passion! What an abomination, what a ghastly disease! The passionate man is an athlete, he knows neither hunger, nor cold, nor exhaustion; he lives miraculously. Passion is Lourdes on a daily basis: look at that paralysed old woman who is wounded in her love—she runs down the stairs with the legs of a twenty-year-old. The passionate man takes no notice of the outside world or of other people; he sees them merely as instruments; the weather, happiness, the neighbour's rights, these things don't exist for him; he knows no obstacles, he overcomes everything; he possesses the patience of an ant and the strength of an elephant. He has no respect for other human beings. Along with fear, passion is the true paroxysm. The passionate man will go and wake up the President of the Republic to satisfy his vice, or, without a moment's hesitation, he will commit all sorts of wrongdoing and go back to sleep, fully placated.

I had great affection for Paul and was very fond of him, but now that he is dead, and after such a long time, I can't help feeling irritated when I think of the atmosphere of passion he built around me. He wore me out, he ruined my health. When Iribe had left Paris for America, I was beginning to be very well known. My emerging celebrity had eclipsed his declining glory. He loved me, subconsciously, when he returned in 193– so as to be free of this complex and in order to avenge himself on what he had been denied. For him I represented that Paris he had been unable to possess and control, from which he had departed in a sulk to join Cecil de Mille, down in his boring, gloomy studios in California. I was his due. He hadn't had me when he should have had me and he intended to take this belated revenge. Too belated for both of us; but it's never too late to mollify those phantoms that we call complexes.

Iribe loved me, but he did so because of all those things that he never admitted to himself, nor admitted to me; he loved me with the secret hope of destroying me. He longed for me to be crushed and humiliated, he wanted me to die. It would have made him deeply happy to see me belong totally to him, impoverished, reduced to helplessness, paralysed and driving a small car. He was a very perverse creature, very affectionate, very intelligent, very self-seeking and exceptionally sophisticated. He would say to me: "You're a poor fool."

He was a Basque with astonishing mental and aesthetic versatility, but where jealousy was concerned, a real Spaniard. My past tortured him.

Iribe wanted to relive with me, step by step, the whole of that past lived without him and to go back through lost time, while asking me to account for myself. One day, he took me to the heart of the Auvergne, to Mont-Dore, to set out on the trail of my youth. We found the house of my aunts … As I walked beneath this avenue of lime trees, I really felt as if I were beginning my life again. I lingered behind. Iribe walked on alone and, on the pretext of finding somewhere to stay, he asked to see my aunts. They had not changed their attitude towards me, after so many years; he was told that if I showed my face, I would not be made welcome.

He came back towards me, soothed and satisfied, having found everything just as I had described it to him. Except that the local people, instead of wearing wool and alpaca, now bought their clothes at the Galeries Lafayette, and the pretty fluted headdresses had disappeared.

Dali jeune

OF THE POETRY OF COUTURE

WORRIED THAT REPORTERS might get bored during the fashion parade, and that certain foreign journalists might not understand my intentions, I decided one day to have a short programme printed for them to explain the collection, provide the numbers of the dresses, and give the price opposite each number etc. The key to the programme was summed up in a few preliminary sentences. In short, a kind of targeted commentary that spoon-fed the press and provided them with a nice, ready-made article that could be despatched that very evening. This programme was a success and the buyers as well as the editors were grateful to me. Couturiers in turn lost no time in adopting this original idea and, as a refinement, began to compile them themselves; they were written not just by artists, but by writers, sometimes even philosophers. The press took them up in the minor key, commented on them, touched them up and made them split hairs.

And in this way the wild lyricism and crazy ramblings that I have called "the poetry of couture" came into being, a type of publicity that was as costly as it was unimaginative and useless.

This lyricism has already begun to manifest itself at the first showing of dresses. The names I heard used in other houses to embellish their collections made me laugh so much that, as a reaction, I just gave mine numbers. Did not my colleague P call one of his creations *Dream of a Young Abbot*? Ridicule can kill many things, but it has never killed the ridiculous.

The poetry of couture has appropriated genius: Claudel, Valéry, Charlie du Bos, Kafka, Kierkegaard, Dostoyevsky, Goethe, Dante and Aeschylus have all been called upon. All they produced were titles such as *Knowledge of Beauty*, or *The Presence of the Couturier*, or *Theories of the Figure*, such as *Pretexts*, *Precedences* and *Approximations*! For followers of Man Ray there was the photographic poetry of couture, for followers of Picasso, with comments by Cassandre, a pictorial poetry of couture, a Dadaist couture, a surrealist couture, while we await an existentialist one. There was Stakhanovite couture: Madame Schiaparelli went and showed her dresses in factories.

The poetry of couture was responsible for cocktails, balls, dinner parties. The champagne flowed, hothouse flowers poured in, we walked about on a floor strewn with orchids.

"If we don't sell well, after that!" sighed L, or P, or W, or M.

If they didn't sell well "after that", it was because it was a failure, or because the crisis proved to be greater than the poetry. For the more the corks popped the more sales slumped. The huge success of the Poiret balls had consequences: a deficit of sixteen million francs.

I have never made a penny out of publicity.

The couture business spent a fortune on maintaining publicity, which is more than nonsense, it's an absurdity, since extravagance damages character. We went back to contrasting colours, which is only tolerable on stage; in town, no woman is sufficiently beautiful for that; with a dress one wears only for ten minutes, you can get away with anything; to wear it all evening is a disaster. You see pockets rising up like udders, buttons that are as big as saucers, adornments in the shape of noses, mouths on the backside, swatches of fur with eyes or hands reproduced on them, lines of Eluard on scarves, and Aragon printed all over handkerchiefs. There again, retribution has not been long in coming: American buyers, whom we used to entice with what was considered to be extraordinary, have fled ('pleasing the Americans' is an obsession of the poetry of couture), for today good taste has passed to the other side of the Atlantic, and the Americans mistrust extravagance and take no notice of these vulgar snares. Marie-Louise Bousquet, Geoffroy and Bérard were the last to realise this. *Marie-Claire*, which should have continued to regard itself as the poor woman's treasure trove, wanted to bolster itself up to the level of *Vogue* and *Harper's Bazaar*. An ordinary woman who wanted to follow *Marie-Claire*'s practical advice step by step would have had to devote five hours a day to her looks.

"You're never satisfied," people will say to me when they read these pre-war aspersions.

I am never satisfied with myself, so why should I be with others? Besides, I like preaching.

And then I have a great sense of modesty. I believe modesty is France's finest virtue. Lack of modesty spoils people for me; I want to restore it to them. When people show lack of modesty to my face, it's as if they were insulting me, as if they were opening my handbag, by force, to rob me.

... I have not done with the poetry of couture ...

By a natural enough transition, this leads me to talk now about inverts. Inverts have had, and continue to have, far more influence on fashion than freemasons do on radicalism, or the Dominicans did on the Front Populaire.

The invert is the enemy of woman, yet at the same time he is haunted by her. When a woman is foolish, she sees in the invert someone who is weak, funny and not in the least dangerous; when she is intelligent, she finds in him someone who can read her, understand her and listen to her; and since all women, simple or subtle, love unctuous compliments and only homosexuals know how to use praise and have the audacity, or the malice, to shower excessive accolades, women are their ideal victims. They are always prepared to believe them. They adore them; furthermore they speak the same caustic language, full of insinuations and appalling traits, and confusingly hypocritical. Inverts don't draw back from anything: they remind me of this story about Madame de Noailles:

"How," people said to her, "could you have complimented that lady on the frightful hat, with its gaudy colours and extravagant shape, which she wore when she made her sensational entrance to your house? Could you really have admired it?"

"I'd prefer anything as long as I didn't have to talk to her about it," Anna replied.

Inverts are always at women's feet: "My lovely, darling, my angel, my enchantress … " They think there can never be too much praise; women do too. They toss garlands of compliments around their necks, strings of flowery flattery, with which they strangle them. Their beautiful lady friends are delighted: women don't dress to please men, but to please homosexuals, and to amaze other women, because they love what is excessive.

"They are charming! They have so much taste!"

They like plucked eyebrows—once they have reassured themselves that they make their rivals look like calves' heads—blond hair that is dark at the roots, orthopaedic shoes that make them look like invalids, their faces laden with foul-smelling grease that will repel men. And should they succeed in having their breasts removed, how they would gloat, Juvenal, how they would gloat!

The number of women I've seen die under the subtle, heady influence of the 'ghastly old queen': death, drugs, ugliness, ruin, divorce, scandal, nothing is too good to destroy the competition and take one's revenge on the woman. Queens want to be women, but they are very bad women.

"They are delightful!"

To get the better of her, they follow her around like shadows everywhere, except to bed; queens work as interior decorators, hairdressers, designers(!), and, above all, as couturiers. They plunge them into a deadly kind of eccentricity, into their artificial hell; in the depths of the abyss I can see them all, my dear friends of yesterday: Béatrix, Florimonde, Clarissa, Barbara, I can name them, count them, but alas not on my fingers.

When I say 'homosexuals', I'm talking about the homosexual spirit, naturally enough, for we all know some excellent, doting fathers, who play the wallflower at dances, who are on the lookout for a good match for their daughters, and who are merely subconscious inverts. Social bodyguards, leaders of decadence, they are the microbes of this gorgeous epidemic, the instigators of truly slanderous hats, the lauders of unwearable dresses, the long-winded and deceitful critics of stiletto heels, the virulent propagators of furniture padded in white satin. They are the only men who like make up and red nails. They form part of the sly, gossip-mongering army of which the cynical, bearded, dirty homosexuals, with their filthy hair in a bun, their gnawed fingernails and their greenish teeth are only the advance guards; they haven't the avant-garde tastes of this old guard, but they maintain the link between it and women; they create the climate. And their favourite vehicle is the poetry of couture.

… And there's no more art of couture! I repeat: couture is a technique, a job, a business. It may be that there is an awareness of art, which is already a great deal, that it excites artists, that it accompanies them in their cars, on the path to glory; that a bonnet with ribbons should be immortalised in an Ingres drawing, or a hat in a Renoir, so much the better, but it's an accident; it's as if a dragon-fly had mistaken Monet's *Waterlilies* for the real thing and had alighted there. If an outfit attempts to match a fine, statuesque body or to enhance a sublime heroine, that's wonderful, but it does not justify couturiers persuading themselves or thinking of themselves—or dressing or posing— as artists … they'll eventually fail as artists.

Three years before the war, I was the target for a great offensive from journalists-poets-couturiers. Their leader, Bébé Bérard, had organised a campaign: he was infuriated by my friendship with Dalí.

Coco à Mote Carlo e 1938

ABOUT WEALTH

M ONEY IS PROBABLY AN ACCURSED thing, but does not our entire civilisation derive from a moral concept based on evil? Without original sin, there would be no religion. It is because it is an accursed thing that money should be squandered.

I judge people according to the way they spend.

I would say to women—never marry a man who has a purse.

Yes, you don't need enthusiasm in order to earn money, you need it in order to spend it. Money that is earned is merely material proof that we were right: if a business or a dress is not profitable, it's because they're no good. Wealth is not accumulation; it's the exact opposite—it serves to free us; it's the "I've had everything and that everything is nothing" of the emperor-philosopher. Just as true culture consists in chucking a number of things overboard; just as in fashion, you generally begin with something that is too beautiful in order to attain simplicity.

I'll return to this when I discuss fashion; I will merely say in passing that one can be elegant and not have money.

But money for money's sake, that grim obsession with wealth, has always struck me as an abomination.

Money is not attractive, it's convenient.

When women love money for what it procures, that's natural, but when they are in love with it, that's appalling. The face of a pretty girl who talks to you about contracts, rent, or life or term assurance becomes so ugly! As for me, I belong to that breed of foolish women, women who think only of their work, and, once work is done, think of fortune-tellers, stories about other people, daily events and nonsense.

The only thing I really like spending is my strength. I would willingly use all my strength in persuading and giving. (A little later on I will tell you that fashion is a gift couturiers make to the age.) It pleases me infinitely more to give than to receive, whether it be at work, in love or in friendship. I have squandered millions. The richest men I have gone out with are those who have cost me the most.

I love buying; the dreadful thing is that once you have bought, you possess. I'm enchanted by small boutiques, haberdashers, second-hand shops, middlemen, clothes dealers. I love antique shops that look like those in Dickens or Balzac's *Peau de chagrin*. Whenever I arrive in a town, I run away from the 'pretty boutique' full of those inept creations I designed ten years previously.

I have a hatred of hanging on to things. I prefer not to have to see the money, the books, the objects, the people that I have lent.

I only care for trivial things, or else nothing at all, because that is where poetry takes shelter. Almost all our emotional, social and moral troubles stem from the fact that we don't know how to give anything up.

Love of money is a physical thing; it's contagious, like a disease. I'm going to tell you a true story, which is rather like a tale by Maupassant. I was staying at my house in Roquebrune, on holiday. I summon my accountant, M Arsène, who comes down from Paris with his lady and his daughter, on the day train, second-class, a respectable gentleman free of any liabilities. M Arsène and his family are my guests for three days. On the third day, once work was over, I discover that M Arsène had bought himself a dinner jacket to come to the South of France and that he didn't want to leave without having worn it for the first time. "Very well, M Arsène, I'll take you to Monte Carlo this evening." We walk into the gaming room.

M Arsène watches the bank notes flying around, the chips piling high, the counters crashing down. Within five minutes M Arsène won as much as his wages for one year. I go off to bed. M Arsène stays behind; he returns the next morning having won a great deal and lost it all. He returns to Paris. Two months later, there was a deficit in the accounts at rue Cambon. It was soon discovered that M Arsène had caught the train back and, on two separate occasions, had come to spend his Sundays in Monte Carlo.

Money adds to the decorative pleasures of life, but it's not life.

It's like jewels. Nothing looks more like artificial jewellery than a very beautiful gem. Why allow yourself to become obsessed with the beautiful stone? You might as well wear a cheque around your neck. A jewel is valued for its bright colours, for its mystique, for its ornamental value—all the values, except those that are reflected in carats. If the jewel is a symbol, an abstraction, then it's the symbol of servility, of injustice or of old age; very beautiful jewellery makes me think of wrinkles, of the flaccid skin of rich old ladies, of knobbly fingers, of death, of wills, of lawyers, of undertakers. A very white earring on the lobe of a well-tanned ear delights me. One day, at the Lido, I saw a respectable, elderly American lady sitting beneath a parasol; all the young American women who were about to go swimming entrusted their jewellery to her; eventually she looked like one of our Holy Virgins in the Auvergne that are festooned with precious stones; the relics of St Mark's paled beside her. "How much more beautiful these young women would be," I thought, "if they dipped their pearls into the waves, into the sea from which they first came; and how brightly their jewellery would glitter if worn on a skin bronzed by the sun, that has lain on the sand!" That distraught stare of envy, those calculating gazes of women who admire the tiaras or bracelets of other women arriving at a party entrance me. I love to lend my jewellery, just as I would lend a scarf or a pair of stockings. I never tire of the pleasure women take in looking at themselves wearing my jewellery, and that sweet smile of gratitude tinged with a longing to kill me ...

Expensive jewellery does not improve the woman who wears it any more than costly fabrics woven with precious materials do; if she looks plain, she will remain so. The point of jewellery is to pay respect to those for whom, and at whose homes, one wears it. I readily wear a lot of jewellery because, on me, it always looks artificial. The mania to want to dazzle disgusts me;

jewellery is not meant to arouse envy; still less astonishment. It should remain an ornament and an amusement. Jewellery should be looked upon innocently, naively, rather as one enjoys the sight of an apple tree in blossom by the side of the road, as one speeds by in a motor car. This is how ordinary people perceive it; for them jewellery denotes social standing. A queen without a tiara is not a queen. In the spring of 1936, a revolution took place in Paris, and at my shop too, in the rue Cambon. I decided to go and talk to the rebels: "Mademoiselle should remove her jewellery!" Angèle said to me, very alarmed. "Go and fetch my pearls," I replied, "I won't go up to the workshops until I have them round my neck." For I was determined to respect the women who worked for me.

SOCIAL WORK

I BEGAN WITH HALF A DOZEN WOMEN working for me. I have had as many as three thousand five hundred.

In 1936, like everywhere else, we had a sit-down strike. (Whoever dreamt it up was a genius.) It was cheerful and delightful. The accordion could be heard playing all over the house.

"What are your demands? Are you badly paid?"

"No." (My staff are always better paid than anyone else's, because I know what work is. Madame Lanvin even accused me of poaching her staff and wanted to take me to court.)

"What are you asking for?"

"We don't see enough of Mademoiselle. Only the models see her."

It was a strike for love, a strike of the yearning heart.

"I want to do something for you," I then said to the staff. "I'm giving you my house."

Grateful thanks from the CGT.[10] Delegations from the trade unions. The new owners set off in search of funds, a working capital, promising to return soon; I'm still waiting for them.

---

10   The *Confédération générale du travail*, the association of French trade unions. [Tr]

At Mimizan, in the Landes, I organised a workers' holiday camp. This experiment costs me millions, which I don't regret. Buildings were constructed to house three or four hundred women. I paid for the travel expenses—second-class, so that they shouldn't be offended—with one month's paid holiday, instead of the legally entitled fortnight.

That lasted for three years. It was lovely, delightful and very jolly, for I didn't want Mimizan to be like a prison.

After three years, the mayor asked me to close down, then he ordered me to do so. The motive: these lone women, he said, were taking away the region's menfolk. The women from the Landes were not able to cope with the situation.

Stravinsky quand il habitait Chez Coco à Garches

STRAVINSKY

In 192– I CAME TO KNOW Stravinsky. He was then living at the home of Pleyel, the older one, in the rue Rochechouart. He was still not very cosmopolitan, and he was very Russian in his ways, with the look of a clerk in a Chekhov short story. A small moustache beneath a large rat-like nose. He was young and shy; he found me attractive. Among this circle, the only man I felt attracted to was Picasso, but he was not available. Stravinsky pursued me.

"You're married, Igor," I told him, "when Catherine, your wife, gets to know … "

And he, very Russian:

"She knows I love you. To whom else, if not to her, could I confide something so important?"

Without being jealous, Misia began to spread gossip. She had sensed that something was happening without her knowing:

"What are you doing? Where are you going? People tell me that Igor walks your dog, explain yourself!"

"I could give a concert at the Salle Gaveau," Stravinsky divulged to me one day, "but I can't afford a sufficient guarantee."

I replied that I would look after it. Ansermet was summoned. Everything was arranged.

"Now," I said to Stravinsky, "you have to speak to Misia about it. Off you go."

Stravinsky goes to see her.

The following day, a Sunday morning, I am setting off to walk around Longchamp.

Misia: "I am overcome with sorrow. When I think that Stravinsky has accepted money from you!"

I had already been through the same "when I think … " in connection with Diaghilev, but in this case Misia feared a catastrophe on quite another scale: that Stravinsky might divorce in order to marry me. Sert became involved. He went and took Igor to one side.

"Môssieu, M Capel has entrusted Madmachelle to me; a man like you, Môssieu, is known as a sh—."

And Misia came back to me, stirring up the drama:

"Stravinsky is in the room next door. He wants to know whether or not you will marry him. He is wringing his hands."

Having said this, the Serts, while cultivating the emotional anguish he was suffering, made fun of Stravinsky. Up until the day when I said to Ansermet:

"It's ridiculous, the Serts are mad. Everyone is talking about this business. Picasso is saying things. I want Igor to come back and for us to be friends."

Stravinsky came back. He came back every day and taught me about music; the little I know about it, I owe to him. He talked to me about Wagner, about Beethoven, his bugbear, about Russia. One day eventually:

"The Ballets [Russes] are leaving for Spain," Stravinsky said to me. "Come with us."

"I will go and find you."

I am on my own in Paris. Grand-Duke Dimitri, whom I had not seen since 1914, arrives in Paris at this moment. We dined together. I saw him the following day. In a very friendly way, I say to him:

"I have just bought a little blue Rolls, let's go to Monte Carlo."

"I have no money, all I've got is fifteen thousand francs … "

"I'll put in the same amount," I replied to the Grand-Duke. "With thirty thousand, we'll have enough to enjoy ourselves for a week."

We set off.

Misia was watching. She immediately sent a telegram to Stravinsky, in Spain: "Coco is a *midinette* who prefers grand-dukes to artists."

Stravinsky almost exploded. Diaghilev sent me a telegram: "Don't come, he wants to kill you."

This affair, which I laugh about today, changed Igor's life entirely. It transformed him. From being shy and self-effacing, it made him, contrary to what would normally have happened, into a hard man with a monocle; from a victim into a conqueror. Like many musicians, Igor has become an excellent businessman, he has a very precise awareness of his rights as an artist and can defend his interests very well.

I fell out with Misia for weeks, following this treacherous telegram. She swore to me that she had sent no such thing. Once again, I forgave her. In any case, Misia turned the wheel of fate, she also turned its page; she intervened, and from that day forth Stravinsky and I never saw each other again.

Étienne de Beaumon

SOCIETY PEOPLE

HERE, I AM GOING TO VENT my anger against the age. Let those who are bored skip the pages. I know that I will sound like the Léon Bloy of couture, but too bad. I am, people frequently say, an anarchist.

I have employed society people, not to indulge my vanity, or to humiliate them (I would take other forms of revenge, supposing I were seeking them), but, as I have said, because they were useful to me and because they got around Paris, working on my behalf; as for me, I went to bed. Thanks to them, I was well-informed about everything, just as Marcel Proust, from the depths of his bed, knew what had been said at all the previous evenings' dinner parties. I know what work is. I have never hired layabouts. Comte Etienne actually slaved away to such an extent that he secretly poached my buyers; he sent them off to his town house where he had set up a second workshop, while still retaining, what's more, the one he had at my house. I dismissed him, for all who are paid deserve hardship. I don't like dilettantes who take other people's place, be it in literature or couture. It is immoral to play at earning one's living.

On the subject of literature, an American newspaper asked me, some ten years ago, for a monthly column along the lines of: "What Mlle C thinks about … " I started writing a few articles; it soon bored me. So I suggested to the editor that he had these pieces done by Princesse Marthe … who writes so prettily that it is almost as if it were Anatole France, from beyond the grave, who was holding Mme Arman's pen on this occasion. Naturally, in these impressions that I was meant to inspire without writing them, I needed to be there myself. From the first article by the Princess of fairy tales, the author had devoted half the column to praise of herself, another quarter to Paris, the City of Light which was intended to be her projector; the rest she used to expose me. "Paris was pink, the colour of pearl, the day was mild, my motorcar drew up in the rue Cambon and I set foot on the pavement: by chance my gaze fell on a pretty yellow sweater; I walked in, filled with wonder at this over-modest and inventive genius among the smaller couturiers who seems to be able to anticipate the wishes of us ladies … " etc. You see the kind of thing. The Princess did not receive her dollars; it was dishonest work.

I have mainly had foreigners work for me. The French have a great facility for asking favours for themselves, but don't want to owe anything to anyone else. (I, on the other hand, like to ask on behalf of others.) When I dressed Parisian ladies without invoicing them, they criticised me, so as to show their independence. Eventually, I paid the bills directly. People said to me:

"Why give them all that money?"

I replied:

"So that they can speak ill of me."

When I took smart friends on a trip, I always paid, because society people become amusing and delightful when they are certain they won't have to pay for their pleasure. I purchased, in short, their good humour. They are irresistibly dishonest. In Berlin, the duchess (an Italian name here), who came with me, had a superb leather coat delivered to the hotel where we were staying, just as we were about to leave. I was in a bad mood, that morning.

"I refuse to pay for that," I said.

"Oh! But there's nothing to pay," replied her boyfriend (for I had brought along the duchess's boyfriend too, of course).

"Why is that?"

"We'll leave without paying. Aurélia didn't give her name … "

It was, after all, like putting something stolen on my account. I like Aurélia very much; she's a great courtesan, four centuries behind her time.

Yes, society people amuse me more than the others. They make me laugh. They have wit, tact, a charmingly disloyalty, a well-bred nonchalance, and an arrogance that is very specific, very caustic, always on the alert; they know how to arrive at the right time, and to leave when necessary.

Having said this, I think it appalling that the wealthy Baronne de R or the very elegant Mrs B should have slept with my colleague P (may God help him!) to procure dresses that they could very well afford; this with the full knowledge of their husbands and lovers, naturally. As far as that goes, I'm an anarchist. If it should continue, and get worse, I'd prefer the Bolsheviks. What's more, a society does not vanish for any mysterious reasons: it crumbles because of little things like that.

Society people have inherited from their forebears a complete ignorance of the most elementary commercial probity; every day is Sunday for them, and everyone is Mr Sunday. As long as they were not involved in business matters, this remained confined to social circles, but nowadays, alas, they are. In the world of couture, I've hardly ever noticed them behaving gallantly any more.

My friend, Madame de V, gave a dinner party for our top couturiers at her pretty Paris home, at which we were all to be seated at small tables. It was, in actual fact, this same P who was to be the guest of honour. The dinner was preceded by a cocktail party in the garden. The hostess was insistent, pressing everyone to stay. I went to her table; I could not find my place, even though I was told I was expected. While I was searching, the other tables, at which my colleagues were presiding, had been filled. I then noticed a little side-table, next to a partition, and I sat down on my own. The maître d'hôtel, who was helping out and who often worked for me, was the first to be aware of my isolation.

"Mademoiselle can't stay there, all alone."

"I'm fine. Bring me some cold chicken."

"Here's some champagne, the real thing, not sparkling wine. For there are two kinds, according to the tables."

I put on my large spectacles and, with great amusement, I looked about me. Surrounding my colleagues, were those glamorous members of Parisian society whom they had dressed. The party was delightful, but I was only too well aware that terror reigned. My women friends would very much have liked to come to my table, out of courtesy, but they didn't dare, for fear of being deprived of their next evening dress.

In short, I was deprived of dessert. The following morning, naturally, my hostess of the previous evening telephoned me to say that she had learnt too late about my punishment, that she was my best friend and that I was head and shoulders above everyone else, and a thousand other exquisitely perfidious pleasantries. All this could only be explained by a need to exaggerate, for, unlike the others, not having anything else to refuse P, this former buyer, she had wanted to do even better, so as to please him.

The kings have gone, but the courtesans remain.

Coco et son amie Lady Abdy

POOR WOMEN

I FEEL SORRY FOR THEM. They are poor creatures. They weren't brought up for this madhouse we live in. They want to vote, smoke, use weapons they know nothing about; they drive lorries; if only they drove them into the ditch! But no, they drive them well, that's the real disaster. They had their grief, their tears, their revolver from Gastinne Renette's, fully paid, but they want more. In their pursuit of man, they have not understood that man adores victims (other people's, of course, not their own).

I feel sorry for women because they always make mistakes. They always bring everything back to themselves. They want to please the passer-by and the passer-by doesn't know this. They don't realise that their virtues (especially if these virtues are masculine ones) cause men to flee.

They conceal their defects instead of considering them as yet another asset. You have to know how to take advantage of your flaws and apply them with cunning; if you know how to make use of them, you obtain everything. You have to hide your virtues if you have them, but people should know they exist. The majority of men are dishonest; all women are.

I don't have friendships with women. Apart from Misia, they never amuse me. They are frivolous, whereas I am thoughtless, but never frivolous. The older I get, the more thoughtless I become. A good-looking woman annoys other women, and she bores men.

A woman = desire + vanity + the need to gossip + a confused mind. Having said this, I adore women's concern for their appearance. So many men, so many poor girls, so many businesses make a living from it! There are many more people who live off women's squandering than people who die from it.

Women choose a dress by its colour; were they not to overlook this essential factor, they would be men. It's all right if they're customers, but it infuriates me to have to open my showrooms to numbskulls whose job it is to look at a collection, but who don't know how to see.

When women see a new dress, they lose their minds. One could smudge the model's white dress ... Women copy men, without realising that what improves a man's appearance, makes them themselves look ugly.

Now here they are grooming themselves at table! They place a gold vanity case, the weight of an ingot, beside their plate and they use their napkin to apply make-up. They put their comb next to their fork. There are blond hairs in the soup. They think their lipstick is a strawberry. They sprinkle the white sauce with ochre. When I see them being served with an escalope, I wonder whether it's to eat or to put on their cheeks.

And in bed! Look at them with their faces covered in black grease that dirties the pillow, with their curlers and their chin supports, and oil on their eyelids. Poor husband! Since she has captured him, it's pointless now to make herself attractive to him; she wants to be attractive to others, those she sees during the daytime, who do not interest her, or who only excite her in so far as they couldn't care less about her. Women are in love with fashion; they would never sacrifice a lover for it. Everybody says to me: "How lucky! You don't put on red nail varnish!" No woman, on hearing that, wants to please them and not use it any more.

Here they are, doomed to the humiliation of having to make advances. Their foot seeks a man's foot beneath the table, and they're only too glad if the foot is not withdrawn. And they complain about not being loved! With their vain chatter, they trap the man into a dilemma: if he's a well-brought-up, reserved man, they will say: "He's a queer." And if he takes any notice of them: "He pounced on me." If women who ought to be giving an example behave like this, think of the others. (Well, the others, fortunately, behave rather better.)

I've never known a man who succeeds because of women. On the other hand, I've known many who have been ruined by women. For many men are judged, unjustly what's more, by their wives. Wives hamper their husbands' careers more often than they further them.

There are many ways of betraying a man and very few ways of deceiving him: foolish or reckless purchases, behaving idiotically, personal hatreds to do with vanity, having bad breath or a poor education. (Whereas deceiving has only one meaning = the carnal sense.) You betray a man by remaining silent at table, like an ass, and by allowing the atmosphere to freeze; you betray him, too, by reciting a few lines you have learnt for the dinner party. By not being in fashion; or by being too much so, by driving lorries, by dressing in printed cotton fabrics, by speaking the jargon of the day: 'getting round someone', 'to have had it up to there', 'OK', 'great', etc. So many women put the man they love in a position of inferiority.

I'm not even talking about the very young, who have an excuse, but about older women, they are the worst. Why do all these former beauties age so badly?

The things they manage to say in front of their husbands defy the imagination: C, the most delightful, the most attractive of our writers, was admiring a statue in my garden.

"How beautiful and restful that character is," he said.

"Have it. I'll give it to you."

"Where are you going to put that?" his wife fumes. "We'll have to move house!"

Embarrassed, he replies:

"I would never take it, but it moves me so … "

(The following day, it is she who comes to take it away.)

"I am happy to give it to you," I say, "because I admire you."

"Oh!" the missus replies in a fury. "If you *will* pay him compliments!"

Now listen to the wife of a well-known doctor; they are talking about how the professor spends his time:

"On Tuesday ... consultation. On Wednesday ... lecture at the faculty. On Thursday ... ah! Thursdays are put aside for love. And I can assure you that the professor does not get bored!"

And now listen to the wife of an industrialist:

"So you think this dress doesn't suit me! I dress badly, no doubt?" (Beginning of the scene, at dinner.)

"One sees too much of your thighs ... " replies M Mathis.

"Do you dare to suggest that you don't like my thighs? They've served you well enough, those thighs!"

All these remarks were overheard on the spot. And they come from the mouths of some of the most prominent women in Paris (none of whom, fortunately for Paris, is a Parisienne. And they're not children, they're people in their fifties!)

I am much more frightened of a woman than I am of a man.

There is also the opposite extreme, which is worse, the scholarly woman, the poetess, the politicised woman.

I prefer a woman who likes blacks to a woman who likes academicians.

The only two female writers who appeal to me are Madame de Noailles and Colette. The Comtesse wanted to dazzle me. She dressed like Cocteau and Cocteau wrote like Anna. She did not eat at table, for fear that she would be interrupted; and when she drank, it was the speaker's glass she held; she would make a gesture with her hand that her sentence was not finished. She looked into my eyes whenever she spoke to me, which pleased me. What is more, I was the only person to recognise that what she said was intelligent.

I like Colette, with her apostle's feet and her accent. But she is wrong to allow herself to get fat. This highly intelligent woman has not understood that it is important to look after yourself. She brags about her greediness. Two sausages would be enough for her; two dozen is affectation. She wanted to astonish Saint-Tropez. And the more embarrassed she felt about her portliness, the more she exaggerated it. Had I been intelligent (and all the more so, had I been an intellectual) I would have been lost; my incomprehension, my desire not to listen, my blinkers, my stubbornness, have been the true causes of my success.

Women never amuse me. I feel no friendship for them. (What is more they don't know what it means.) In France, in any case, friendship is a challenge.

The word 'honour' has no meaning for women.

They don't play the game, but they expect it to be played with them.

Couples are the worst.

You can like them individually; together, they are detestable. As for being the friend to both of them, it's like squaring the circle. The couple is an association; an association, 'unity is strength', is tiresome because it is useful. Love should be an organisation for mutual extermination and not a charity. It's just as difficult to witness complicity in a couple as it is dissension. The couple never stop to think of the intolerable position of a third party; a couple is never straightforward, generous and spontaneous; it is nothing but reflection, scheming and selfishness. It's inhuman: it's an artificial creation, a corporation. Even if the couple loathe one another, they unite against you; it's like one of those serrated wheels that bite into one another, but make the machine function better.

But fortunately "the woman is not always the female of the male; there can be two completely dissimilar people in a household". It was Balzac who said that; it's comforting. Marie Laurencin used to say: "I detest that third person who is known as the Couple."

Boy Capel would often say to me:

"Remember that you're a woman ... "
All too often I forget that.

So as to remind myself, I stand in front of a mirror: I see myself with my two menacing arched eyebrows, my nostrils that are as wide as those of a mare, my hair that is blacker than the devil, my mouth that is like a crevice out of which pours a heart that is irritable but unselfish; crowning all that, a great knot of schoolgirl's hair set above the troubled face of a woman who spent too much time at school! My dark, gipsy-like skin that makes my teeth and my pearls look twice as white; my body, as dry as a vine-stock without grapes; my worker's hands with cabochons that resemble an imitation American knuckle-duster.

The hardness of the mirror reflects my own hardness back to me; it's a struggle between it and me—it expresses what is peculiar to myself, a person who is efficient, optimistic, passionate, realistic, combative, mocking and incredulous, and who feels her Frenchness. Finally, there are my gold-brown eyes which guard the entrance to my heart—there one can see that I am a woman.
A poor woman.

ON FASHION
OR: A GOOD IDEA IS MADE TO PERISH

FASHION SHOULD BE DISCUSSED enthusiastically, and sanely; and above all without poetry, without literature. A dress is neither a tragedy, nor a painting; it is a charming and ephemeral creation, not an everlasting work of art. Fashion should die and die quickly, in order that commerce may survive.

At the beginning of creation, there is invention. Invention is the seed, it's the germ. For the plant to grow, you need the right temperature; that temperature is luxury. Fashion should be born from luxury, it's not twenty-five very elegant women (dressed, incidentally, free of charge, which is not luxurious), luxury is first and foremost the genius of the artist capable of conceiving it and giving it form. This form is then expressed, translated and disseminated by millions of women who conform to it.

Creation is an artistic gift, a collaboration of the couturier with his or her times. It is not by learning to make dresses that they become successful (making dresses and creating fashion are different things); fashion does not exist only in dresses; fashion is in the air, it is borne on the wind, you can sense it, you can breathe it, it's in the sky and on the highway, it's everywhere, it has to do with ideas, with social mores, with events. If, for example, at this moment, there are no indoor dresses, none of those tea-gowns beloved of the heroines of Paul Bourget and Bataille, it is probably because we live at a time when there is no longer any indoors.

I have created fashion for a quarter-of-a-century. Why? Because I knew how to express my times. I invented the sports dress for myself; not because other women played sports, but because I did. I didn't go out because I needed to design dresses, I designed dresses precisely because I went out, because I have lived the life of the century, and was the first to do so.

Why have the ocean liners, the salons, the big restaurants never adapted to their real purpose? Because they are conceived by designers who have never seen a storm, by architects who have never been out in the world, by interior decorators who go to bed at nine o'clock and dine at home. Similarly, before me, couturiers hid away, like tailors, at the back of their shops, whereas I lived a modern life, I shared the habits, the tastes and the needs of those whom I dressed.

Fashion should express the place, the moment. This is where the commercial adage 'the client is always right' get its precise and clear meaning; that meaning demonstrates that fashion, like opportunity, is something that has to be grabbed by the hair. I am looking at a young woman on her bicycle, with her bag on her shoulders, one hand placed chastely on her knees that rise and fall, the material of her clothing cleaved to her stomach and chest, and her dress puffed up by the speed and the wind. This young woman has developed her own fashion, according to her needs, just as Crusoe built his hut; she is admirable and I admire her. I admire her so much that I don't see another woman who approaches me at full speed. She crashes into me, we fall down together, and I find myself on the ground with my face between her two bare thighs: it's wonderful. She yells at me, it's perfect.

"So what were you looking at?" she says to me.

"I was looking at you, Madame, to make sure I was not behind the fashion."

For fashion roams around the streets, unaware that it exists, up to the moment that I, in my own way, may have expressed it. Fashion, like landscape, is a state of mind, by which I mean my own.

"This dress will not sell," I sometimes tell my staff, "because it is not me."

There is a Chanel style of elegance, there was a 1925 or 1946 elegance, but there is no national fashion. Fashion has a meaning in time, but none in space. Just as there are Mexican or Greek dishes, but no authentic cuisine in these countries, there is a regional type of clothing (the Scottish plaid, the Spanish bolero), but nothing else. Fashion came from Paris, because for centuries everybody used to meet there.

Where then does the couturier's genius lie? The genius is in anticipating. More than a great statesman, the great couturier is a man who has the future in his mind. His genius is to invent summer dresses in the winter, and vice versa. At a time when his customers are basking in the burning sun, he is thinking of ice and of hoar frost.

Fashion is not an art, it is a job. If art makes use of fashion, then that is sufficient praise.
It's best to follow fashion, even if it is ugly. To detach oneself from it is immediately to become a comical character, which is terrifying. No one is powerful enough to be more powerful than fashion.

Fashion is a matter of speed. Have you visited a fashion house just before the collection is shown? Something I made at the beginning of the collection, I may find outdated before the end. A dress that is three months old! A collection takes shape during the final two days; in this respect our profession is like the theatre; how often does a play only come together between the rehearsals and the final dress rehearsal? Ten minutes before the buyers arrived, I would still be adding bows. At two o'clock in the afternoon, we would still be trying dresses on the models, to the despair of the manager of the fitting rooms, who is responsible for organising these pretty performers' manoeuvres.

If the role of the fashion designer is reduced by you to so little, to the blithe and brisk art of capturing what's in the air, don't you think it's only natural, people say to me, that others do the same, that they copy you and draw their inspiration from your ideas just as you were inspired by ideas that were scattered around Paris?

But of course—once an invention has been revealed, it is destined for anonymity. I would be unable to exploit all my ideas and it's a great pleasure to me to discover them realised by others, sometimes more successfully than me. And that is why I have always differed from my colleagues, over the years, about what for them is a great drama, and which for me does not exist: copying.

Working in secret, seamstresses searched every evening on leaving the workshops, counterfeit proceedings, spies, samples that vanish, patterns that are fought over as if they contained the secrets of the atomic bomb, all that is pointless, puerile and ineffectual. I began with two collections a year. My colleagues embarked on four of them, so as to have time to copy mine. ("Only better," they used to say; and occasionally they were right.)

What rigidity it shows, what laziness, what unimaginative taste, what lack of faith in creativity, to be frightened of imitations!

The more transient fashion is the more perfect it is. You can't protect what is already dead.

I remember an evening at Ciro's where there were seventeen Chanel dresses, not one of which was made by me. The Duchesse d'Albe greeted me with these words: "I swear that mine came from you." It was quite pointless. And this was what the Duchesse de La Rochefoucauld said to a friend, whom she had invited there with me: "I don't dare meet her, my Chanel dress did not come from Chanel's." I retorted: "I am not really sure myself any more that my own dresses are made by me."

It is because fashion must move on that its fragile existence is entrusted to women. Women are like children; their role in everyone's eyes is to use things up, to break, and to destroy: an appalling turnover. It is essential for those industries that only exist because of them. The great conquerors measure themselves by the ruins they leave behind them.

I only like what I create and I only create if I forget.
So, a little over ten years ago, the big fashion designers ganged together and formed an 'exclusive' club known as the PAS (Protection des Arts saisonniers) which, under the guise of a league against copying, was a trust. Was it really necessary for twenty or so favoured fashion designers to prevent forty-five thousand from earning their living?

What can these little designers do if not interpret the big ones?

To have to take out a patent for a dress, even less, for a drawing, just as one would on a brake for a quick-firing machine-gun, I repeat, it's not modern, it's not poetic, it's not French. The world has lived off French inventions, and France, for her part, has lived off the development and shaping of ideas invented by other people; existence is nothing more than movement and change. If these couturiers are the artists they claim to be, they should know that there are no patents in art, that Aeschylus did not have a copyright and that the Shah of Persia did not sue Montesquieu for infringement. Orientals copied, the Americans imitated, the French reinvented. They have reinvented Antiquity several times: Ronsard's Greece is not Chénier's; Bérain's Japan is not that of the Goncourts, etc.

One day, in 192– at the Lido, because I was growing tired of walking barefoot in the hot sand, and because my leather sandals were burning the soles of my feet, I had a shoemaker on the Zattere cut out a piece of cork in the shape of a shoe and fit two straps to it. Ten years later, the windows of Abercrombie in New York were full of shoes with cork soles.

Weary of carrying my bags in my hand and losing them, in 193– I had a strap attached and wore it on my shoulder. Since then …

Jewellery from jewellers' shops bores me; I had the idea of getting François Hugo to design clip-on earrings, brooches, and all that fancy costume jewellery that one sees today even in the galleries of the Palais-Royal and the arcades on the rue de Rivoli.

I would be sad if all those little things had a brand name. I've given life to all that, but if I had wanted to protect myself, I would have given my own life.

I wonder why I embarked upon this profession, and why I'm thought of as a revolutionary figure? It was not in order to create what I liked, but rather so as to make what I disliked unfashionable. I have used my talent like an explosive. I have an eminently critical mind, and eye too. "I have very certain dislikes", as Jules Renard said. All that I had seen bored me, I needed to cleanse my memory, to clear from my mind everything that I remembered. And I also needed to improve on what I had done and improve on what others were producing. I have been Fate's tool in a necessary cleansing process.

In art, you always have to start out with what you can do best. If I built aeroplanes, I would begin by making one that was too beautiful. You can always do away with it later. By starting out with what is beautiful, you can always revert to what is simple, practical and cheap; from a finely made dress, revert to ready-made; but the opposite is not true. That is why, when you go out into the streets, fashion dies its natural death.

I often hear it said that ready-made clothes are killing fashion. Fashion wants to be killed; it is designed for that.

Cheap clothes can only originate from expensive ones, and in order for there to be low fashion, there must first be a high one; quantity is not just quality multiplied, they are essentially different. If that is understood, if people are aware of it and admit it, Paris is saved.

"Paris will no longer create fashion," I hear people say. New York will invent it, Hollywood will propagate it and Paris will be subjected to it. I don't believe that. Of course, cinema has had the same effect on fashion as the atomic bomb; the ratio of the explosion of the moving image throughout cinemas knows no bounds on Earth, but I, who admire American films, am still waiting for studios to impose a figure, a colour, a style of clothing. Hollywood can deal successfully with the face, with the outline, the hairstyle, the hands, the toenails, with portable bars, refrigerators in the drawing-room, clock-radios, with all man's repercussions and knick-knacks, but it doesn't deal any more successfully with the central problem of the body, which it has not managed to disassociate from man's inner drama, and which remains the prerogative of the great designers and ancient civilisations. At least until now.

The Americans have asked me countless times to go and launch a fashion show in California. I have refused, knowing that the outcome would be contrived and therefore negative. There are much richer terrains than stony Burgundy or sandy Guyenne; from Persia to the Pacific they have tried to make wine, but they have never succeeded in creating the red wine of the Clos-de-Vougeot, or Vin d'Aÿ. Wealth and technique are not everything. Greta Garbo, the greatest actress the screen has given us, was the worst dressed woman in the world.

A well-known manufacturer of Lyonnais fabrics grabbed hold of me on my way through Lyon.

"I'm going to show you something that will revolutionise dressmaking," he said to me.

And he brought out some cartoons printed on silk.

"I've bought the rights from Walt Disney," he announced proudly. "What do you think of that?"

"You're wasting your money on inanities," I replied.

"Aren't you keen on the idea?"

"I'm very frightened of ridicule. Walking along with a cow on your behind, it's there for all to see. I am all for what is unseen. Keep your fabrics. They'll make charming nursery-room curtains. Would you dress your wife like that?"

"Ah! No. 'My sovereign'" (that's what he called his wife) "cannot wear such things."

Colleagues will say to you:

"Chanel lacks daring. Chanel is a revolutionary who has been overtaken by the revolution."

I would reply that there can be revolutions in politics, which is a poor thing (since there are but two solutions, ever since the world began, to man's ability to live in society, liberty and dictatorship, solution A and solution B) and which has only a semi-circle in which to move, a right and a left; but that there can be no revolution in couture, which is something rich, subtle and profound, like the social mores of which it is an expression.

To sum up, prêt-à-porter clothing exists. There is some marvellous prêt-à-porter. Prêt-à-porter has triumphed, and it is already flooding the world, but to mix quantity with quality, is to add apples to pears. France will be the last to be conquered. Paris never will. Our country is too small for prêt-à-porter. Our exiguity rescues us. Citroën thought he was Ford; he came from Holland, he did not understand that Grenelle was not Detroit.

And to go back to imitation in dressmaking, I have asked my colleagues: can they copy us freely abroad? Yes. Do they? Yes. Then it's totally pointless to take out a patent on a dress. It's admitting you have run out of ideas. And if you relent against the big international sharks, why take the bread out of the mouths of our little couturiers? Racine and Molière never had to put up with teachers. Along with plagiarism go admiration and love.

People have loathed me for defending this thesis, I've been boycotted and I've been deprived of raw materials for seven years. But my thesis is as good today as it was yesterday.

If I have dwelt on this argument about copying, it's because it has created a gulf between my colleagues and me that has never been filled. However much I might introduce new fashions or designs, bring about new manufacturing processes, and keep vast industries alive, the world of couture has not understood a thing. Man is born a bureaucrat, you can't change him. He codifies everything; he dykes up all the rivers and religions end up in green files.

Do you see what a foul temper I really have?

I admire and love America. It's where I made my fortune. For many Americans (whom we don't know, and neither do I), I am France. I think I would be better understood there than anywhere else, because America does not work 'for Americans'; that is to say, like our French couturiers do, with their gazes fixed on *Life* and *Fortune*. Present-day America is overpopulated with French people, with writers, professors, politicians and journalists. Have American fashions been influenced in the slightest way? There is luxury in America, but the spirit of luxury still resides in France. I know what luxury is. For ten years I lived in the world's greatest luxury. Why go and look for American or English models, as Molyneux does? Why go to New York to look for a style that is brought back to Paris and transformed? A dress is not like those Bordeaux wines that travelled round the world and which would improve during their crossing by sailing ship.

People in the trade are not meant to think about eccentricity, but quite the reverse, to remedy whatever there may be that is excessive. I prefer what is too respectable. You have to use what is at your disposal; a woman who is too beautiful upsets others, and one who is too ugly depresses the strong sex.

There are five intelligent women in a million: who can say this to them, if not a woman?

Women think of every colour, except the absence of colours. I have said that black had everything. White too. They have an absolute beauty. It is perfect harmony. Dress women in white or black at a ball—they are the only ones you see.

Customers are solely interested in detail; they can't concentrate. They are wrong to disregard men's opinions. For men love to go out with well-dressed women, but not when they are conspicuous. If their partner looks conspicuous, they prefer to stay at home, to avoid the agony of being stared at. Why are women not content simply to please, but have to surprise? Only very young men need to have their happiness spelled out to them, for the crowd to turn round as their partner passes by.

Revolutions in fashion should be conscious ones, the changes gradual and imperceptible. I have never started off with a preconception, with an abstract idea; I have never decided ten months beforehand that dresses would be worn longer the following season.

I have never had actresses as customers. As far as fashion is concerned, actresses no longer existed after 1914. Before that, they dictated the fashion.

le Duc de Westminster

A LAST KING

O NE DAY, PAMELA, the Englishwoman who worked for me, came and said to me (we were in the South of France):
"Do me a favour. It won't cost you anything. If you do it for me, I shall be given a present. I want a present or, more precisely, I need one. Westminster has just arrived. His yacht is lying at anchor off Monaco. He wants to meet you. I have promised, in exchange for a reward, to take you to dine there."

I liked this all too unusual plain-speaking, but it didn't disarm me. I was accustomed to Pamela, accustomed to seeing women purely as monsters.

"I certainly won't go."

I beg you!'

"I won't go."

Soon afterwards, with my usual spinelessness, I had relented. Pamela would have her present. I agreed to have dinner the following evening. During the daytime a telegram arrived from Paris, sent by Dimitri, informing me that he would actually be arriving next day. I cancelled my appointment, naturally. When Dimitri turned up, I told him about this, in front of Pamela.

"Had I been invited, I would very much have enjoyed seeing this yacht," said Dimitri in a delightfully casual way.

"That's fine, I'll arrange for you to be invited," said Pamela, immediately spotting a solution.

Two hours later, Westminster invited the grand-duke to dinner that same evening.

"Dimitri, you were wrong … " I said.

"Why?"

"I don't know. But one shouldn't force fate. Somehow I feel that you might have done better to have dinner alone with me … "

Ten years of my life have been spent with Westminster. I will describe later on what those years were like. First, I'm going to describe the man, because the greatest pleasure he gave me was to watch him live. Beneath his clumsy exterior, he's a skilful hunter. You'd have to be skilful to hang on to me for ten years. These ten years were spent living very lovingly and very amicably with him. We have remained friends. I loved him, or I thought that I loved him, which amounts to the same thing. He is courtesy itself, kindness personified. He still belongs to a generation of well-brought-up men. All Englishmen, for that matter, are well brought up, until they reach Calais at least.

Shortly before the war, I was invited to dinner at the house of M Jean Prouvost, the editor of an important evening newspaper. Being very punctual, I arrived at his home at 8.45 pm, the appointed time. On the pretext of a headache, M Prouvost had his guests wait for two hours. We had to wait to sit ourselves down at table. M Prouvost didn't even apologise. The lessons in good behaviour that he was being given at the time by a little high society lady had been of no use to him at all.

To behave badly in an elegant way, you first have to have been well brought up. This was the case with Westminster.

He is simplicity made man, the shyest person I've ever met. He has the shyness of kings, of people who are isolated through their circumstances and through their wealth. Because he is thought to be among the most important men in England, he is embarrassed by this; he knows people know; he would be no less embarrassed if he wanted to prove that he is a man like all the others. Westminster hates meeting people, and he avoids first encounters. Unless he manages to bypass the obstacle and get past unwittingly, with his head down, in which case, once the danger has been overcome, he looks a happy man. I caught sight of him one day in Biarritz, coming out of a bar, holding, in a familiar way, the arm of a man who was talking to him garrulously and with gay abandon.

"Do you know who he is?" I asked Westminster when he had rejoined me.

"Not at all."

"He's Poiret, the couturier."

"A good fellow!" said Westminster, delighted.

The following day he came across Poiret at the tennis club, greeted him in the most friendly manner, and came over towards me, gloating.

"You know," he said, "your Poiret didn't intimidate me in the least."

I mention this characteristic, because it is like those you come across in memoirs; it could belong to Louis XVI, Charles VI, or a child king.

Westminster is elegance itself—he never has anything new; I was obliged to go and buy him some shoes, and he's been wearing the same jackets for twenty-five years. Nothing would make him go to the tailor, or receive a visit from him. Westminster owns two yachts: a Royal Navy reserve destroyer and a four-master. When you arrive on dry land, all the guests are wearing splendid yachting caps to go and buy postcards in the port. He never disembarks except in an old soft hat.

Westminster is the richest man in England, perhaps in Europe. (Nobody knows this, not even him, especially not him.) I mention this firstly because at such a level wealth is no longer vulgar, it is located well beyond envy and it assumes catastrophic proportions; but I mention it above all because it makes Westminster the last offspring of a vanished civilisation, a palaeontological curiosity who naturally finds a place in these memories. Showing me over the luxurious surroundings of Eaton Hall, one of Westminster's residences, Lord Lonsdale said to me:

"Once the owner is no more, what we are seeing here will be finished."

It is as dreadful to be too rich as it is to be too tall. In the first instance you don't find happiness and in the second you can't find a bed.

Westminster has a delightful temperament, provided you don't bore him. He gets bored enough on his own as it is. He's a corpulent chap, heavy, robust, at least on the outside. His intelligence lies in his keen sensitivity. He abounds in delightful absurdities. He does harbour a few grudges, petty elephant-like grudges, which he keeps simmering because he's a tease. He doesn't much care for human beings, but mainly likes animals and plants.

At Eaton Hall, in Cheshire, as I walked in the grounds, I discovered, hidden away in a valley, some greenhouses that were as big as those that belong to the City of Paris. They grew food, for every season, peaches, nectarines, strawberries … just as they once did in Russia or in Poland.

I took Westminster there. He didn't seem to be aware that he owned all that; we pounced on the strawberries, picking them like schoolchildren. The next day I wanted to go back on my own to the greenhouses; the doors were locked. I told my good friend about this, and he had the head gardener summoned.

"I locked the greenhouses because some thieves had stolen some strawberries, my lord," said the gardener.

"The thieves … it was Mademoiselle!" replied Westminster feebly.

The gardener had spent his life at Eaton Hall and it had never occurred to him that his master might, even playfully, eat strawberries straight from the bed.

We went back to the greenhouses, on another occasion:

"What beautiful flowers!" exclaimed Westminster. "Where do all these magnificent orchids go? Why do we never see them at the house?"

"They go to hospitals, to the church … " replied the head gardener.

I admired the way these immense fortunes became anonymous and were swallowed up in the community, as a river that is too broad seeps into the sands.

In spite of the greenhouses, Westminster only really liked natural flowers, and he continued to do so. What gave him greatest pleasure was to bring me the first snowdrop, picked from the lawn, in a box.

Westminster has houses everywhere. On every new trip, I discovered them. He is far from knowing all of them: be they in Ireland, in Dalmatia, or in the Carpathians, there is a house belonging to Westminster, a house where everything is set up, where you can dine and go to bed on your arrival, with polished silverware, motor cars (I can still see the seventeen ancient Rolls in the garage at Eaton Hall!) with their batteries charged, small tankers in the harbour, fully laden with petrol, servants in livery, stewards and, on the entrance table, always scattered everywhere, newspapers, magazines and journals from all over the world.

The money spent on periodicals that are delivered here and which no one reads would provide me with income enough, a Scotsman, an old friend of Westminster's, said to me.

On the moors of Scotland, the grouse are ready to be shot, or the salmon to be fished; at the same moment, in the forest of Villers-Cotterêts or in the Landes, the stalkers who track the wild boar or stags have only to saddle their horses to prepare the way and pick up the right scents; you have to wonder whether they sleep in their red clothes, or whether the captains of the yachts, which are always under sail or being pressurised, are not in reality painted onto their poop-decks, and, in short, whether this absurd fairyland (which isn't even intentional, but which exists because that's the way it has been, for generations) is not a bad dream, a tramp's dream.

Eaton Hall is on the outskirts of a pretty town (Hester, which belongs to His Grace), in Shakespeare country, full of black and white half-timbered houses with pointed gables from the time of

Falstaff. All that is left of the castle, which defended the Roman frontier against the Welsh for a long time, are its medieval cellars, for it resembles Walter Scott Gothic; it is surrounded by Italian-style terraces, training routes for horses from the studs, model farms, forests of rhododendrons as in the novels of Disraeli, and galleries where the Rubens, the Raphaels, the English masters and the Thorvaldsens are all the rage.

Why did Westminster like me?

Firstly, because I had not tried to lure him. English women think only of luring men, all men. If you have a very famous name and are immensely rich, you stop being a man and become a hare, a fox. Every day is the opening of the hunting season. In these sorts of situations, you can imagine how restful it is to live with someone you have pursued yourself, someone who the next day, probably, will dig a hole under the cage and run away.

English women are either pure spirits ('souls'), or grooms. But in both cases they are huntresses; they either hunt with horses or with their souls, but it's always a chase. In my case, it's never occurred to me to say: "There's a man I like, I'll catch him, where's my gun?" Sport has become second nature to many English women, but first of all comes man.

Aurélia rides very well; she has the reputation of always being behind her dogs. One day, on horseback, I said to her:

"So jump then!"

"Oh! no! I'm too frightened, alone with you … I'll only jump if there's a man to watch me. It's not worth it, just for you."

Westminster liked me because I was French. English women are possessive and cold. Men get bored with them. (American men, on the other hand, can't stand French women; they never, or hardly ever, marry them. Whereas there are countless French women who have been successful in England.)

Besides, English women are not entirely disinterested. French women used to be, they're not any longer. (You mustn't accuse me of running down English women. Firstly, I run everybody down; secondly, what I am saying collapses in those mirrors of social customs that are English novels; especially bad ones, of which I've read so many; bad novels paint a much more striking picture of society than good ones do.)

We, ourselves, are not to blame if English women are gauche; if they only do things that displease men. The English are a breed of horse. At the races, or playing cards, they're horses. Swift saw it very clearly. Do you remember, in *Gulliver*, in the land of the Houyhnhnms, the two horses that converse by saying *"Houyhn, houyhn"*?

I said all this once in an article that caused a stir in London. The article was by Randolph Churchill; he had submitted it everywhere and it had been turned down. I went along with him to the *Daily Mail*: the article appeared on the front page, at the time of Ascot. I only mentioned English men, with gentle humour. Not a word about women. It was a great success: all the men fought over it.

Tilly, a Frenchman who, at the end of the eighteenth century, wrote some of the most pertinent and impertinent things about the English, made this extremely accurate remark: "The English are the best people in the world at marrying their mistresses and asking them least about their past."

As to friends.

There was Churchill.

There was the tiny Duke of Marlborough, whom I called Little Titch, alongside his giraffe-like mother. He said of his wife: "The duchess thinks she is the most refined of all women."

There was Lonsdale.

My friends bored him. He couldn't understand Misia at all, and she couldn't understand England at all. He was appalled by Sert, who sawed off swans' beaks so that they would die of hunger, and who pushed dogs into the Grand Canal in Venice.

It was not my destiny to become an Englishwoman. What is termed an 'enviable situation' is not one for me. I insisted that he got married.

I grew bored, with that squalid boredom that idleness and riches bring about. For ten years, I did everything that he wanted. A woman does not humiliate herself by making concessions.

I always knew when it was time to go.

It can drag on for months, a year, but I know that I will go; I am still there and already I'm absent. I had satisfied a great core of lethargy that hides beneath my activity; I had wanted to be a woman from a harem, the experiment was terminated. Fishing for salmon is not life. Any kind of poverty is better than that kind of wretchedness. The holidays were over. They had cost me a fortune, I had neglected my house, deserted my business, and showered gifts on hundreds of servants.

I could have been the richest of women, in the most precise use of the word. Every day my friend would say to me: "Take all those Rembrandts", "Those Frans Hals are yours".

He said to me:

"I have lost you. I won't be able to get used to living without you."

I replied to him:

"I don't love you. Do you enjoy sleeping with a woman who doesn't love you? The men I have been brutal with have immediately become very sweet."

Westminster suddenly saw that I was no longer there.

With me he realised that he could not have everything he wanted, that being His Grace meant nothing as long as a little Frenchwoman could say no to you; it was a shock for him; it threw him off balance.

Several years later, Westminster invited me to stay. I was travelling in Italy at the time. I replied to him: "I shall be a guest. Be very kind to me." I returned to Scotland. My friend had taken up with his circle of parasites once more.

I was unlucky. The trip was not a happy one. After the sun-drenched Lido, it was raining in London. There was no longer a secretary waiting at St Pancras station. Westminster did not meet me in Inverness. It was a dry summer; there was no water in which to fish.

"What changes!"

A Frenchwoman from the provinces ...

She had decided to make the house smart!

There were no longer any guns or fishing rods in the front hall.

I had written to his wife beforehand: "If you would prefer me not to come, I won't go." "Not in the least," she replied, "I know your methods (why not my recipe or my martingale?) I know you won't speak ill of me."

From the heights of his wealth, Westminster knew the tedium of the peaks, the loneliness of the great tyrants, that condition of being beyond the law that accompanies the man for whom nothing is impossible. I didn't dare complain of feeling unwell, or say that I had a migraine, because immediately, someone would make a phone call and the most famous specialists would arrive from Harley Street with their medicine bags, after a journey of twenty hours, and all for nothing, since I refused to see them. I stopped venturing to express a wish, because the magic carpet would bring it, or make it happen, before I'd completed my sentence, with the speed of a shooting star.

Amused by the contrast of our type of hunting and hunting as it is practised in England, for example, I mentioned one day, in the course of a mundane conversation, that it would be lovely to show Eaton Hall to the retinue Westminster maintained in the Landes. Straight away, the thirty Frenchmen, grooms and whippers-in, stepped ashore, having spent the night in the English Channel. He travelled the seas like a monarch, as the white Royal Navy ensign was saluted by warships and fluttered over the underground lakes of oil in Gibraltar.

And all that, to what end: boredom and parasites.

Cora Chanel en 1938

ADIEU, NOT AU REVOIR

I HAVE TRIED TO TALK ABOUT MYSELF, without thinking of me. For any human being who thinks of himself or herself is already dead. But since, when others no longer think of you, you are also dead, I have reluctantly decided to place myself on stage and impose my presence upon you.

My life has been merely a prolonged childhood. That is how one recognises the destinies in which poetry plays its part. I have never forgotten anything. I have emerged totally ignorant and fully prepared from the depths of the Auvergne. I have never had the time to think of being unhappy, of existing for another human being, or having children. It is probably not by chance that I have lived alone. I am born under the sign of the Lion; astrologers will know what that means. It would be very difficult for a man, unless he were strong, to live with me. And it would be impossible for me, were he stronger than me, to live with him.

The finest gift God has given me is to allow me not to love those who do not love me. And to have left me unaware of the most common form of love, jealousy.

I am not a heroine. But I have chosen the person I wanted to be and am. Too bad if I am disliked and unpleasant.

What I have told you expresses my faults better than it does my virtues. I have a few virtues, reasonably charming ones; I am full of impossible faults. As I've told you at the beginning, I am all pride. Unless I am mistaken and I am merely vanity; true pride not only does not admit itself, but does not even describe itself; it's the pride of Louis XIV, or that of the English temperament.

It would be sufficient to hear me to realise quickly that I lack balance, that I talk too much, when it's easy to please by listening, that I forget quickly, and furthermore, that I like to forget. I throw myself at people in order to force them to think like me.

Changing one's mind appals me. Listening to others irritates me, except when eavesdropping; what they say gets on my nerves from the very first sentence, and yet I have an inexplicable liking for pointless discussion, which exhausts me. I work willingly amid noise, conversation, activity and confusion. I try hard to make myself attractive when I talk, I think as I talk, I construe as I talk.

I am neither intelligent, nor moronic, but I don't think I'm an easily categorised character. No one is in France, for that matter. I've conducted business, without being a businesswoman. I've made love, without being a loving sort of woman. I think that the only two men I have loved will remember me, on earth and in heaven, for men always remember a woman who has caused them a lot of anxieties. I have done my duty towards people and life without any axiom, but because I like to see justice done.

People believe that I exude rancour and malice. They believe … Well, they believe anything, apart from the fact that one works, one thinks of oneself and one takes no notice of them. I am a good person, provided that I am not told that I am one, for that bores me stiff and irritates me. Because I am irritated, irritable and irritating.

I provide contrasts that interest me alone, but which I cannot manage to get used to—I think I am the shyest and the boldest person, the gayest and the saddest. It's not I that am violent, it's the contrasts, the great opposites that clash within me. I hate to be complaining, yet I like to complain and play the victim. I shun medicine, yet I have a passion for pharmaceutical products, because pharmacists are interested in what I have to say, whereas doctors don't listen to me.

I am not in the least frivolous. I have a boss's soul. I take everything seriously. I am sincere in everything. I have never drawn a cheque on my own account without being able to cover it.

I have a horror of loneliness and I live in total solitude. I would pay so as not to be alone. I would have the duty police constable sent up in order not to dine alone. And yet I only expect ingratitude from people. (True generosity is perhaps to experience ingratitude and to accept it.) But if I let myself slip,

I know that melancholy awaits me, open-mouthed … Boring people are poisonous and boredom has the same effect on me as a devastatingly lethal poison. Goodness annoys me and reasonableness bores me to tears.

Every time I've done something reasonable, it's brought me bad luck.

Anyway, that is the person I am. Have you understood? Very well, I am also the opposite of all that.

These are the materials that my memory has supplied me with, together with the bits and pieces that have been thrown into my garden and the motes that I have found in my neighbour's eye.

What I am telling you is not a testament.

Where I am to go now, I don't know, but I'm going somewhere and it's not over. I have seen the approach of what has happened sufficiently clearly to be able to guess what will happen next. When people tell me that Europe is in ruins, I feel that she is my mother and that I shall stay close to her; but when they add, which is rather more serious, that Europe is old-fashioned, I feel that I would not be sorry to leave her, just as I left my family, and that I would continue or begin my life again very well without her.

If the Europe that is to come were to be the opposite of the one we are leaving, I would adapt myself to it; if, on the other hand, it's the same Europe, only poorer and grimmer (I was going to write uglier, but it's not that), then I'm off. "But fashion is Paris!" people say to me. I reply: provided that Paris is Paris and Europe is Europe. But Paris will not be Paris, nor Europe, Europe, as long as customers prefer a sausage to a dress and as long as I see American officers in uniform arriving at my shop … people who are in reality former clients, officers whose colonel is likely to throw his arms around my neck and tell me his name is Madeleine Carroll.

I believe that what will happen in the world tomorrow, will not happen in Europe. There's the real tragedy. For I want to be part of what happens. I will go wherever is necessary for that. I am prepared to wear out entire societies with my efforts, just as one wears out a horse.

It will be necessary to go elsewhere. It will be necessary to do something else. I am ready to start all over again.

Away with death! Hold on to life! (I have a keen interest, nevertheless, in the other side. I shall go to paradise to dress real angels, having created my hell on earth with the other angels.)

In any case, I shall never rest during my lifetime. Nowhere would I worry as much, or exhaust myself as much, as in a rest home. I am well aware how bored I would get in heaven, even on an aeroplane I get more bored than I do on the ground.

It's not Europe that interests me, it's the earth revolving. My tormented little face of a Jivaro Indian, which disappears beneath my hair when I look at myself in the mirror, strikes me as the image of telluric convulsions.

I have been a couturier, by chance. I have made perfumes, by chance. I am now going to tackle something else. What? I don't know. Here again, chance will decide. But I am quite ready. I am not saying goodbye for long. I am not thinking of anything, but when the moment comes, I feel I will pounce on something that will be within my reach.

For a quarter-of-a-century, I have created fashion. I will not begin again. It's the age that is in chaos, not me.

I have never known failure. I have succeeded totally in everything I have undertaken. I have done more good turns for people than I have bad ones. I have thus acquired moral well-being, as well as the other kind. That has made me free as a bird. However much M Sartre may explain to me that I am pitiful, cooped up in my human condition (as Lassalle said, in the early days of Marxism: "You first make the worker understand how unhappy he is"), I have decided to be happy without requiring that daily dose of poison, recently invented, that we call happiness.

I have been responsible for some wonderful and useful inventions: I have been reviled, as much by those they have impoverished as by those they have enriched.

I had a girlfriend whom I adored, she betrayed me.

I have spread goodness around me as much as I could and in return only received slaps in the face.

I have tried to improve the lot of the women who work for me and no good has come out of it.

I have loved two men, and when it came down to marrying

them, all I tried to do was marry one of them off and make the other one settle down.

I have dressed the whole world and, today, it goes about naked.

All of that delights me. All of that satisfies this deep taste for destruction and evolution that is within me. Life is recognisable through its inconsistencies. The world is nothing but struggle and confusion. Contrary to what Sert used to say, I would make a very bad dead person, because once I was put under, I would grow restless and would think only of returning to earth and starting all over again.

TRANSLATOR'S AFTERWORD

W HAT WAS GABRIELLE CHANEL really like? Several biographies have been published in France, notably the highly fanciful one by Edmonde Charles-Roux, *L'Irregulière* (Grasset, 1974), published in an almost impenetrable English translation as *Chanel* (Cape, 1976; reprinted by Quercus, 2009); and no less than three celebrated writers—Paul Morand, Louise de Vilmorin, and Michel Déon—have patiently withstood Chanel's renowned volubility and have attempted to tell her life story, according to what she chose to reveal, in her own words.

With the reopening of her Paris premises in rue Cambon in 1954, 'Coco' Chanel, then aged seventy-one, considered it necessary to provide her public—particularly the wealthy American market—with an 'official' record of her life that would help bolster her newly-revived post-war reputation. Yet her true purpose was twofold: firstly to perpetuate her own self-created myth and expunge her wretched, poverty-stricken childhood by creating one that she could embroider and adapt to her own taste; and secondly, to avenge herself on a public that had all too quickly forgotten her after the debacle of 1940 and, in many cases, had not forgiven her for her sentimental allegiances during the Occupation.

Louise de Vilmorin's unfinished account—begun in Venice, during Chanel's exile, in the autumn of 1947, but only finally published in book form, after Vilmorin's death, as *Mémoires de Coco* (Le Promeneur, 1999)—was not to Chanel's liking, particularly after the manuscript failed to attract a contract from an American publisher. It is a book that reflects its author as much as it does its subject, for Louise de Vilmorin was a formidable figure in her own right and her meetings with Coco Chanel must have been a clash of Amazon-like proportions. Louise was also an intimate friend of Duff Cooper, the British ambassador to Paris at the end of World War II, who, at Winston Churchill's behest, protected Chanel and thus saved her from the *épuration* ('cleansing') —the fate of many French women who had been intimately involved with German officers.

Michel Déon first caught sight of Mademoiselle Chanel before the war, at the Monte-Carlo-Beach hotel, where his father had pointed her out to him walking in silk pyjamas beside the swimming-pool, followed by the Duke of Westminster smoking an enormous cigar: "Look at that lady there, she is Mademoiselle Chanel, and behind her, that large man in shirt sleeves, with his trousers all twisted, and his old yachting cap, that's one of the richest men in the world and the cousin of King George V.""[11]

Déon did not meet this "exceptional, and at the same time exasperating and brilliant woman", however, until November 1952, in Roquebrune-Cap Martin, on the French Riviera, when he first began helping her to write her memoirs. In his

---

11   Michel Déon *Pages françaises* (Gallimard 1999)

own captivating autobiographical work, *Pages françaises*, he describes the month he spent at her Villa La Pausa, where his duties included driving Mademoiselle Chanel to lunch with Jean Cocteau at Cap-Ferrat. But Déon's main duties as 'ghostwriter' really began in 1953. Chanel was living in post-war exile at the Beau-Rivage Hotel in Lausanne, as she had sold her property, and for over a year she paid Déon to take down her confabulated memories of her miserable childhood in the Auvergne, her early success, the famous people she had known (Stravinsky, Dalí, Picasso, Cocteau, etc); her intimate friendships (Arthur 'Boy' Capel, the Duke of Westminster, Grand-Duke Dimitri, Paul Iribe, though not, interestingly enough, the true love of her live, the poet Pierre Reverdy). Déon persevered, rewrote a number of chapters, and after a year or more produced a three-hundred-page manuscript born of Chanel's lengthy monologues. But the book was still not to her taste. Déon believes that she may have had a childlike fear of abandoning the world of her dreams and confronting the realities of existence, for she said nothing to him, but sent word via a friend, Hervé Mille, the editor of *Paris-Match*, who conveyed her reaction: "In these three hundred pages, she says there is not a single sentence that is not hers, but now that she sees the book as it is, she thinks that it is not what America is expecting."

Paul Morand first met Gabrielle Chanel through Misia Sert in 1921, as he describes in typically limpid style in his preface to this book. They were both stars of their generation: she, the undisputed queen of fashion; he, a young diplomat and the author of such acclaimed books as *Tendres stocks* (a collection of stories with its preface by Marcel Proust) and the novel, *Hecate and Her Dogs*. Cosmopolitan, refined, effortlessly accomplished, Morand reflected a certain idea of Third Republic France, one that would vanish forever with the disaster of the German occupation. "Everywhere I go, they are switching out the lights," he once remarked to Michel Déon.

Morand, who was an admirer of English traditions and literature, and who had many friends in England, had been working in the French embassy in London from 1939 to July 1940 as 'chief of the blockade commission'. Influenced possibly by his Germanophile and anti-Semitic Roumanian-born wife Hélène, he made the fateful decision to return to France in July 1940 and to support the 'wait and see' government of Maréchal Pétain. In 1943 he was appointed Minister in Bucharest, and in 1944 'Plenipotentiary Minister' in Berne. It was in Switzerland, along with many another political exiles, that he was obliged to take refuge after the war, and it was from his home in Vevey in 1946 or 1947, impoverished and vilified by much of the French literary establishment,[12] that he was invited by Coco Chanel to visit her in St Moritz and offered the opportunity to write her memoirs. We do not know what Mademoiselle Chanel thought of her friend's efforts, or indeed whether Chanel ever read his manuscript—it was put away in a drawer and only came to light again, after Chanel's death, in 1975. *L'Allure de Chanel* was finally published in Paris in 1976, the same year that Paul Morand died, and, for the first time, readers were at last given

---

12   Morand's candidature to the Académie Française was effectively vetoed by de Gaulle in 1958; he was finally elected and presumably 'forgiven' in 1968.

some insight into the woman Chanel really was. Just occasionally in these selective, acid-tongued memoirs, the mask drops, and we glimpse the true face of the fragile, lonely creature who revolutionised the way women dress and who became one of the twentieth century's great *monstres sacrés*.

In her biography of Paul Morand, published in 1994, Ginette Guitard-Auviste quotes from a letter Morand sent to her in response to a question she had asked about Chanel. "Chanel is France's greatest figure," he wrote from Vevey on 1st May 1964. "Despite her age, she sparkles; she is the only volcano in the Auvergne that is not extinct... the most brilliant, the most impetuous, the most brilliantly insufferable woman there ever was."

EUAN CAMERON

TRANSLATOR'S NOTE

I should like to thank Raphaëlle Liebaert, Koukla Mac-Lehose and Nelly Munthe for their good advice and suggestions, and I am especially grateful to Michel Déon, a friend to both Coco Chanel and Paul Morand, for his generous hospitality in Galway and for guiding me through certain of Mademoiselle Chanel's more abstruse and puzzling allusions.

Michel Déon's own fleeting but unforgettable glimpses of the formidable former 'queen of the rue Cambon' in his memoir *Pages françaises*, read in conjunction with *The Allure of Chanel*, provide, in my view, the most authentic portrait we have of this extraordinary woman.

EC

PHOTOGRAPHIC CREDITS